Fo

GRAN

POCKET ANNUAL 1995

Bruce Smith

Mark Eames

Photography

Bryn Williams and Colin McMaster

1st Year of Publication

Formular 1 Grand Prix Pocket Annual

ISBN: 1-898351-25-2

First published in April 1995 by
Words on Sport Ltd

Words on Sport Ltd
PO Box 382, St. Albans,
Herts, AL2 3JD

Typeset by Bruce Smith Books Ltd

Photographs:
Bryn Williams, Colin McMaster

Disclaimer

In a book of this type it is inevitable that some errors will creep in. While every effort has been made to ensure that the details given in this annual are correct at the time of going to press, neither the editor nor the publishers can accept any responsibility for errors within.

Registered Office:
Worplesdon Chase, Worplesdon,
Guildford, Surrey, GU3 3LA
Reg. No.: 2917013

Repro by Ford Graphics, 8-10 Whitsbury Road, Fordingbridge, Hampshire, SP6 1BR
Tel.: (01425) 655657

Printed by Bell and Bain Ltd., Glasgow

CONTENTS

Review 94 and Statistics

A-Z Formula 1 Drivers

Team Directory

Circuits Directory

Race Diary

Introduction

This is the first edition of the *Words on Sport Formula 1 Grand Prix Pocket Annual,* a sister publication of the *Motor Racing Yearbook*. It is a unique publication and provides within its pages a complete review, preview and guide to the 1995 season. Complete driver and team details are provided along with a guide to all the circuits proposed for the 1995 campaign. Full details of the 1994 season are also given along with a comprehensive list of F1 records. If you are lucky enough to travel to the circuits of the World in person or are equally engrossed from your armchair you should find everything you need to enhance your viewing and settle the odd argument or two. If you feel something is missing then do drop us a line or eMail on the addresses below:

Words on Sport, PO Box 382, St. Albans, Herts, AL2 3JD, England.
Fax International: +44 1923 894366   Fax England: 01923 894366
eMail Compuserve: 100126.103

The Editors would like to thank all the Formula One Grand Prix teams for their co-operation in producing this annual.

Headlining Changes

Formula One Grand Prix racing made the headlines for all the right and wrong reasons in 1994. The Drivers championship title race that was, at times, bitterly fought out on and off the tracks of the world, had everyone glued to their armchairs around the globe as suspensions and bans ensured it ran right to the last race if not to the chequered flag itself. After over a decade of safe racing, time as always caught up and fatalities took their toll and deprived the sport of major players. As always though the authorities were quick to move and the sport's governing body – the FIA – imposed immediate changes and enforced them rigourously. As the season climaxed in the Australian summer further changes were already planned and during the short close season design teams have complied and innovated to produce safer and potentially more exciting races. We shall see.

Car Rules

The changes to the FIA rulebook have laid stringent parameters for teams' car designers to work in, with figures detailing aerodynamics, dimensions, capacity, weight and engines now cast in stone. The changes which are outlined below in strictly laymans terms have in effect changed the emphasis of car design from aerodynamics to structural safety. The trade-off for improved driver safety is effectively a loss in speed, which should mean slower lap times and a greater importance placed on tyre management as the wear will be much greater. This is a small price to pay (as is any price when it comes to life and death matters) and could lead to even more exciting tactical races in terms of pit-stop strategy.

The aerodynamical changes have effectively cut the amount of available *downforce* by nearly a third. After the deaths of Ayrton Senna and Roland Ratzenberger at Imola, the FIA introduced the use of a 10mm plank under the car, thus forcing teams to raise the car off the ground to accommodate the plank. This allowed more air to travel under the car and thus have the effect of decreasing the difference in pressure between the top of the bar and the bottom (like aircraft wings working in reverse) and reducing the downforce (and grip) on the road. Further changes in the body design of a car have reduced this downforce even further by reducing the size and effectiveness of the front and rear wings. The 10mm plank has been supplemented with the introduction of a a 50mm stepped chassis, a safety measure used in IndyCar racing. The plank has been retained to prevent the introduction of ultra-stiff suspension as a means of getting the car body closer to the ground. Measured in G-terms, drivers will now expect to pull about 0.4G less than the 3G they were experiencing around a fast corner in 1994.

At the front of the car the depth of the nose wings has been reduced to 200mm while the maximum height of the main wing at the rear is 800mm when measured from the lowest point on the chassis.

The power of the engines used in F1 has also been reduced by reducing their size from 3.5litres to 3.0litres and limiting them to a maximum of 12 cylinders. Indeed as you will see from the car specifications detailed in the teams section of this annual many teams are running engines with 10 or even eight cylinders. Turbo-chargers are strictly outlawed and standard 'pump' fuel is now adopted in place of the specifically mixed concoctions used previously and this is one of several areas that will be strictly monitored by the FIA. The governing body has announced that they will take regular samples of fuel from teams competing in both the qualifying and race stages and these will be analysed in a chemical unit that will attend all races to ensure that they match the pre-season specimens supplied and approved by the FIA.

One change in the rulebook that did light up car designer' eyes was the freeing of the fuel tank capacity, where the minimum restrictions have now been lifted. Designers have now been able to reduce tank size with a view of producing a car with better weight distribution. This capacity reduction will make it impossible for cars to complete a full race without refueling stops, but as regular tyre stops look to be as imperative now, a three stop race strategy could become the norm.

Another measure that was introduced last season that has also been retained for 1995 is pressurising the engine by venting the airbox at high speed.

Electronics as always play a part in engine and transmission control and these were strictly monitored during 1994. With reduced downforce available there is even greater emphasis on traction control as the better it is the faster corners can be taken and accelerated out of. Electronic traction control is not allowed, but 'fly-by-wire' throttles are, but will no doubt be strictly controlled by the FIA who will carry out on-the-spot checks. However, problems here seem likely as this will mean the teams having to give details of the software which controls this highly sensitive area of car control systems.

Various restrictions apply on the use of semi-automatic gearboxes but electronic clutches are allowed. With the extra space provided by reduced fuel tank capacity the opportunity for designers to revert to longitudinal gearboxes has arisen although not all teams have adopted this approach and some may retain a transverse six-speed gearbox. To prevent wheels flying off, each must now have a spring retention clip fitted.

The most visible changes though are in the driver accommodation which will make their survival shells just about as safe as they can be and prevent a lot of crash related injuries particularly in the protection of the head and neck. The minimum length of the cockpit opening has been increased by 150mm to 650mm and there must be a minimum distance of 50mm between the front of the cockpit surround and the steering wheel. This change makes the use of steering wheel shrouds impossible and should ensure that drivers cannot hit the front of their helmets on the chassis when crashes or shunts occur as they inevitably will. Lateral head protection is also facilitated by a 150mm increase in the minimum height of the cockpit to 550mm.

A minimum distance of 750mm between the front of the cockpit and the front wheel axle line has also been imposed on designers and this has meant that the driver pedals are behind an axle line drawn between the two front wheels. In addition the length of the deformable structure in front of the driver's legs is at 300mm now double its original length and has lead to a slender-looking design on most cars. Housed inside this protective cone must be an impact absorbing structure which is tested to meet pre-set criteria laid now by the FIA. In addition the driver's headrest must rise to a height of at least 75mm above the seat.

What will be the nett effect of these changes in car performance? As already mentioned lap times are likely to be a few seconds slower than in recent years due to the reduction in downforce. A power loss of about 100 hp would be likely because of the 0.5 litre reduction in engine capacity however, most engine designers are likely to counter this by running engines at a much higher speed – thus expect that many cars will be running at and probably beyond 15,000 rpm.

Races are likely to retain the tactical stance that played such an important role in the the 1994 championship with fuel stops. Reduced tank capacities will ensure this interesting aspect of racing continues but with increased emphasis placed on tyre selection and changes.

All-in-all, after the trials and tribulations of 1994, 1995 really promises to be an exciting year for Formula One. As always, there will still be points of controversy and debate, but that is good for the development of the sport. But now the driver really does come first and if the season ends with those who strated it still present, unharmed and uninjured – then Formula One really will have entered a renaissance era. *BS*.

Using the Annual

The *Formula 1 Grand Prix Pocket Annual* is divided into several clear sections that arrange information, statistics and reviews in relevant sections which are clearly defined in the Contents list on page 3.

At the start of each section you may find a small guide or key to specific information and abbreviations used.

Through the Pocket Annual a set of country abbreviations are used and the key to these is listed below. Thus *Jap* signifies a Grand Prix in Japan.

Key to Races

Arg	Argentina	Jap	Japan
Aus	Australia	Mex	Mexico
Aut	Austria	Mon	Monaco
Bel	Belgium	NZ	New Zealand
Bra	Brazil	Pac	Pacific
Can	Canada	Pes	Pescara
Dal	Dallas	Por	Portugal
Esp	Spain	SA	South Africa
Eur	Europe	San	San Marino
Fin	Finland	Swi	Switzerland
Fra	France	USA	United States of America
GB	Great Britain		
Ger	Germany	USAE	United States of America (East)
Hol	Holland		
Hun	Hungary	USAW	United States of America (West)
Ita	Italy		

Review '94

"No pun intended but we are playing with fire. I don't know whether it is more dangerous or not because I simply sit in the car at refuelling but if there is a spillage it can obviously catch fire and the prospects of a spillage increase when people are working flat out" – Damon Hill.

March

For the second season running the Formula One circus arrived at Interlagos in Brazil minus the reigning World Champion – Alan Prost's decision to retire following on from Nigel Mansell's switch to Indy Cars twelve months earlier. The new season promised to deliver a thrilling sixteen race series – triple World Champion Ayrton Senna was finally sitting in a Williams-Renault partnering Damon Hill. Michael Schumacher and the Benetton team were threatening to come good and an unknown Peugeot engine joined forces with the established McLaren set-up, and there was the promise of a return to form by the Ferraris of Jean Alesi and Gerhard Berger.

Three of the big four, Williams, Benetton and Ferrari, filled the first four places on the grid with Heinz-Herald Frentzen's Sauber and the Footwork of Gianni Morbidelli making up the top six. It was Michael Schumacher who recorded the first victory of the season as he led Damon Hill's Williams home by 36 seconds. Senna had led on home soil before being passed by the Benetton, before spinning out on lap 55 admitting after the race that he had been pushing too hard. Jean Alesi picked up a podium finish behind Hill, with Rubens Barrichello's Jordan, the Tyrrell of Yuko Katayama, and Karl Wendlinger's Sauber taking places four, five and six respectively.

In the post race inquest the FIA hit Jordan driver Eddie Irvine with a one race ban and a $10,000 fine after he was found to be responsible for a four car accident on lap 34 involving Jos Verstappen, Eric Bernard and Martin Blundell. On appeal the governing body lifted the fine but increased his race ban to three. Despite FIA president Max Moseley promising a clamp down and stringent penalties on teams and drivers who brake the rules, Irvine's punishment for his dramatic *'racing accident'* seemed excessive.

April

The TI circuit in Aida staged the first of two Grand Prix that would be held in Japan during the season and marked the inauguration of the Pacific Grand Prix. The Ferrari team is the next to upset the FIA after revealing that it had run an illegal *'power reduction'* system in one of the practice sessions.

The McLaren-Peugeots of Mika Hakkinen and Martin Brundle found themselves in the top six on the grid with Schumacher, Berger and both the Williams. Senna failed to finish again this time making his exit on the first lap after a nudge from Hakkinen had pushed the Brazilian into the path of Nicola Larini's Ferrari – Larini deputising for the injured Jean Alesi. Damon Hill joined his team-mate back in the pits on lap 49 with transmission failure.

This left Schumacher to bring his Benetton-Ford home three-quarters of a minute ahead of Gerhard Berger's Ferrari who was the only other driver to finish on the same lap. Rubens Barrichello came home for his first ever podium finish in his Jordan-Hart, with Christian Fittipaldi fourth in the Footwork, the Sauber of Heinz-Herald Frentzen fifth, and Erik Comas in the Larrousse sixth. Martin Brundle saw his chance of third place evaporate 16 laps from the end of the race when his new Peugeot engine failed to go the distance.

May

The San Marino Grand Prix at Imola will be remembered as the blackest weekend in the history of Formula One – Ayrton Senna and Roland Ratzenberger killed after separate crashes, Rubens Barrichello lucky to walk away from the wreckage of his Jordan and four mechanics injured by a flying wheel. Events in the principality would have a drastic effect on the motor racing world with the loss of life leading to questions of the sport's safety and future.

The weekend had started with Rubens Barrichello being thrown into a tyre barrier when his car lifted into the air after touching a kerb. Miraculously, Barrichello suffered no more than a cut lip and a sprained arm – unfortunately worse was to follow. Eight years since the death of Elio de Angelis during a private practice session, the sport was forced to come to terms with the death in final qualifying of Simtek driver Roland Ratzenberger. It had been the Austrian's dream to compete in the World Championship as a Formula One driver, but his car went out of control as he came through the Gilles Villeneuve bend, and he hit the wall at over 200km/h.

After much soul-searching the race went ahead despite the death of Ratzenberger, and there was surprise that the red flag did not appear at the very start when the Lotus of Pedro Lamy ploughed into the back of

JJ Lehto's Benetton which had stalled on the grid – the pace car came onto the circuit while the wreckage was cleared. However, the red flag made a numbing appearance on lap five following a fatal crash which deprived the sport of one of the all-time greats. Brazilian Ayrton Senna had clinched three World Championships driving in a style that had made him a legend in Formula One history, as well as a national hero in his home country. Entering the Tamburello just ahead of Schumacher's Benetton, Senna's Williams continued in a straight line and hit a concrete wall at over 200kmh. After witnessing Ratzenberger's crash the day before, and despite the monocoque of the Williams remaining intact, nobody realistically expected Senna to survive. He was airlifted to the Maggiore Hospital in Bologna and his death was announced at 1740 local time.

Whether the race should have re-started is a decision that will continue to be debated but nevertheless Michael Schumacher went on to complete a hat-trick of wins ahead of the Ferrari of Nicola Larini who completed his first points finish in his 44th start. The last act of the fateful weekend saw the rear wheel of Michele Alboreto's Minardi fly off as he exited the pits. Four mechanics, three from Ferrari and one from Lotus, were slightly injured. Mika Hakkinen's McLaren was third, with Wendlinger, Katayama and Hill in fourth, fifth and sixth respectively.

The deaths of Senna and Ratzenberger were to have implications for all the Formula One teams for the rest of the season, with the FIA immediately announcing new technical regulations and mindful of a world audience. The teams themselves were not pleased, saying that the governing body had over-reacted and announced the changes without adequate thought. With concerns about the safety of the circuits as well as the cars, the Grand Prix Drivers' Association was formed to give the drivers a greater say in the sport.

With the memory of Imola still in the minds of all those connected with the sport, the stage moved to Monaco where F1 suffered another numbing blow as at the end of the first qualifying session Karl Wendlinger's Sauber crashed leaving him in a coma and fighting for his life. The popular Austrian was in the thoughts of the drivers as they gathered on the grid to stand and pay their respects to Senna and Ratzenberger on the day of the Monaco Grand Prix. Wendlinger's team mate Heinz-Herald Frentzen withdrew from the event as his mark of respect.

Damon Hill's race was complete before the end of the first lap. His Williams collided with the McLaren of Mika Hakkinen. Gianni Morbidelli's Footwork and the Minardi of Pierluigi Martini were also casualties on the first lap. At the front of the field, Michael Schumacher continued in Benetton's quest to win every race of the season as he took the chequered flag 37 seconds ahead of the McLaren of Martin Brundle, with Gerhard Berger in a Ferrari third. Jean Alesi, returning after injury, was fifth sandwiched between the Jordan of Andrea de Cesaris, making the most of replacing the banned Eddie Irvine, and the Minardi-Ford of Michele Alboreto.

The month of May was completed with the Spanish Grand Prix in Barcelona where Michael Schumacher's dominance was finally ended – only because the German found his Benetton stuck in fifth gear for two-thirds of the race! It was also the first time that some of the new FIA regulations came into effect with the aerodynamics of the cars altered so as to reduce the amount of downforce.

The race was also significant in that it saw the debut of Scotsman David Coulthard who had stepped up from test driver to fill the enormous gap left by Ayrton Senna. He qualified ninth but went out of the race on lap 32 with an electrical fault. On lap 23 Schumacher's gear problems started and it was a testament to his driving abilities that he was able to continue let alone finish second behind Damon Hill. In the 42 laps he had left to race, he kept in touch with Hill despite having to pull away from two pit stops in a highly inappropriate gear. Martin Brundle came home in third to give the Tyrrell-Yamaha a podium finish with Jean Alesi fourth, Martini fifth and Eddie Irvine, returning from his three race ban, in sixth.

June

The Canadian Grand Prix in Montreal saw the introduction of further changes to the rules following the nightmare of Imola. After those made to regulate downforce in Barcelona, adaptations were made to reduce the horsepower of the cars with modifications to their air boxes, and the teams were also required to use standard fuel.

Benetton, Williams and Ferrari dominated the circuit as they had done in practice. Schumacher took his fifth win in six races ahead of Damon Hill. The Ferraris of Jean Alesi and Gerhard Berger were third and fourth, with David Coulthard scoring his first ever points in fifth and JJ Lehto picking up sixth having started 19th on the grid. Brazil's Christian Fittipaldi in his Footwork had initially been credited with the one point, but he was disqualified after the race because his car was found to be underweight.

13

Both McLarens failed to complete the race distance of 69 laps with Martin Brundle out on lap four with electrics. *Engine failure* was with the cause of Mika Hakkinen's retirement seven laps from the end. With six races of the season gone, Schumacher's lead over Hill was an impressive 33 points and the talk was now of what was coming – not what had gone.

July

The start of July and the French Grand Prix in Magny-Cours saw the return of a familiar face in the Williams-Renault. After winning the Indy Car Championship in his rookie year, Nigel Mansell was tempted by Frank Williams back to Formula One, who knew that the 1992 World Champion was not happy in his second season with the Newman-Haas team. Mansell would race in France for a rumoured £1 million as the Didcot team looked for a high profile replacement for Ayrton Senna. The deal struck with the Briton would also see him compete in the last three Grand Prix of the year after the Indy Car season was complete.

For the first time this season Michael Schumacher's Benetton was not on the front row. Damon Hill had the edge over guest team-mate Nigel Mansell as the German could only manage third ahead of the Ferraris and the Jordans. Despite his disadvantage, Schumacher made a blistering start as he headed both Williams drivers into the first corner. The Benetton and the lead Williams of Hill started their own battle ahead of Mansell who maintained third place up to lap 45 when he retired with transmission problems.

Schumacher went on to record his sixth win in seven starts with Hill coming home thirteen seconds adrift. Gerhard Berger was third, with the two Saubers, in only their second season in Formula One, both finishing in the points by sandwiching the Minardi of Pierluigi Martini.

A week later and the half way stage of the 1994 season was reached with more drama, as well as considerable confusion, at the British Grand Prix at Silverstone. Qualifying offered little excitement with Hill ahead of Schumacher on the grid for his home race with the Ferraris of Gerhard Berger and Jean Alesi on the second row. Berger picked up a $10,000 fine after he broke the pit lane speed limit after his cars speed limiter failed to work. David Coulthard was sitting back in the second Williams after Nigel Mansell had returned to the States. He was seventh on the grid, but stalled at the start of the parade lap, and was forced to start the race from the back of the grid.

The parade lap was also to have severe implications for championship leader Michael Schumacher. A seemingly innocuous incident went unnoticed by the majority of the spectators at Silverstone as his Benetton passed the pole car of Damon Hill, and although they were back in formation as they lined up for the start of the race, it was a breach of the rules by the German.

On lap 13 it was announced that Schumacher would receive a five second penalty but it was not suggested that this would take the form of a stop-go penalty. Schumacher continued to race only to be black flagged – which he claimed after the race he did not see. Hill went on to win the race in front of his own fans with Schumacher second. But hours after the race had finished Schumacher was disqualified for ignoring the flag and fined $25,000. Alesi was promoted to second ahead of Mika Hakkinen who had collided with fourth placed Rubens Barrichello on the last lap. David Coulthard picked up his second points finish ahead of the Tyrrell of Ukyo Katayama.

Benetton took Schumacher's disqualification to appeal, and 27th July turned out to be an eventful day in Paris for a number of other teams and individuals. Schumacher's disqualification for the British Grand Prix was upheld and he was also banned for two races for ignoring the black flag. On top of this, his Benetton team was fined $500,000 for failing to adhere to the instructions of the officials over the black flag incident. Benetton were also hit with a further $100,000 fine along with McLaren for being slow in providing information about redundant systems in their electronics systems relating to banned technology. Pierre Aumonier, who was the clerk of the course at Silverstone, had his Superlicence suspended for failing to perform his duties adequately over the weekend of the British Grand Prix, and McLaren's Mika Hakkinen and Jordan's Rubens Barrichello each received a one race ban, suspended for three races, for failing to speak to stewards following their coming together on the final lap.

An eventful month was to continue at Hockenheim as the season entered its second half in Germany. Benetton had taken Michael Schumacher's two race ban to appeal, and until his case had been heard, the German was free to race on home tarmac. The Ferraris of Berger and Alesi delighted when they excelled on the circuit best suited to their powerful engines as they occupied the front row of the grid ahead of Damon Hill and favourite Schumacher.

On lap 15, with the race in full flow, Schumacher's Benetton team-mate Jos Verstappen came into the pits for a routine pit stop. His tyres were changed, but whilst refuelling, around four litres of fuel spilt over the hot car. It ignited, engulfing the pit crew as well as sending up a column of fire spiralling 35 feet in the air towards guests in the VIP viewing area above the pit lane. The fire was quickly extinguished by the mechanics and safety marshals, but the incident left Verstappen and a number of mechanics with minor burns, and horrified the spectators and the watching millions on television.

This all followed on from the green light where eleven cars had crashed out at the first corner after the start of the race. Sauber, Lotus, Minardi and Jordan lost both their cars with Brundle's Tyrrell, Hakkinen's McLaren and the Ferrari of Jean Alesi also crashing out. Whilst everyone was looking for the red flag to appear, the race proceeded, and it soon became clear that the race was to continue without almost half the field. With so many cars already out of the race, it was not surprising that only eight cars finished the 79 laps.

The German crowd saw the Ford engine of their heroes Benetton fail for the first time in nine races, and Gerhard Berger went on to complete Ferrari's first win since Spain back in 1990. It was also a good weekend for Ligier and Arrows, with Olivier Panis and Eric Bernard both finishing on the podium to record their highest ever placings for the French team, while Christian Fittipaldi and Gianni Morbidelli came home in fourth and fifth respectively ahead of the two Larrousse cars of Erik Comas and Olivier Beretta. Damon Hill was the last of the finishers but well out of the points.

Mika Hakkinen was blamed for the first corner incident and was subsequently banned for one race and therefore McLaren, who did not contest the decision, would be looking for a replacement driver for Hungary in two weeks time. Alessandro Zanardi, Michele Alboreto and Andrea de Cesaris each received a suspended one race ban for not talking to stewards after the first corner skirmish.

August

August began with yet more controversy and Benetton in trouble with the sport's governing body yet again – this time over the fire at Hockenheim. It was revealed that Benetton had removed a filter from the refuelling equipment in order to speed up the delivery of fuel into the car. Benetton insisted that they had been given permission to remove the filter, and later changed their story to put the blame on a mechanic who had removed it without permission. The team was found guilty of tampering with the refuelling equipment by the World Motor Sport Council, but escaped any punishment.

In the Hungarian Grand Prix at Hungaroring, Philippe Alliot replaced the suspended Mika Hakkinen with David Coulthard securing his best starting position of third behind Michael Schumacher and Damon Hill who once again occupied the front row of the grid.

The two Jordans managed to get one bend further in Hungary than they did in Germany before they combined with Katayama's Tyrrell to take an early walk back to the pit lane while the race went on around them. The scene at the front of the race was a familiar one with Schumacher taking the chequered flag over twenty seconds ahead of Hill, with the World Championship leader's team-mate Jos Verstappen putting the nightmare of the fire in Germany behind him as he claimed his best ever Formula One result with a podium finish. Martin Brundle's McLaren took him seventy-six laps in fourth as he, along with the Tyrrell of Mark Blundell and the Ligier of Olivier Panis, finished one lap down but in the points.

If Benetton thought their season could get no worse, then they were wrong. With Schumacher's failed appeal against his two race ban, the Belgian Grand Prix at Spa-Francorchamps represented the German's last chance for points until mid-October. His weekend started with the Jordan of Rubens Barrichello snatching pole off him, as the Brazilian took advantage of the break in the rain at the end of the session to put in a tentative fast lap on quicker tyres on a track that was still extremely wet in places. However, Schumacher swept past the Jordan on the first lap as the race got under way, and the German was already on his way back to his home in Monaco with the winner's trophy when stewards back in Belgium were announcing his disqualification to the remaining news media.

According to the rules the 10mm plank under the car was allowed to be reduced by 1mm during a race. The plank under Schumacher's Benetton had a depth in places of 7.4mm, and therefore according to the FIA's Technical Director Charlie Whiting, was infringing the rules. Hill inherited the win and a further four points, bringing him to within 21 points of Schumacher with the German banned from the next two races in Monza and Estoril.

Mika Hakkinen returned from his ban to take a belated second, with Jos Verstappen taking a second successive podium finish – although he never actually stood on it! The second Williams of David Coulthard was fourth, with Mark Blundell's Tyrrell fifth and Gianni Morbidelli sixth in his Footwork. Gerhard Berger picked up a suspended one race ban for pulling off the circuit in a dangerous manner after his race was ended on lap 11 when his engine blew.

The month ended as it had started in controversy with the FIA upholding their decision to ban Michael Schumacher for two races following the now infamous black-flag incident at Silverstone. The German would be missing for the next two races in Italy and Portugal, and following the German's disqualification at Spa, Damon Hill has the chance to close the gap in the World Championship to just a single point should he win both races. It made compulsive viewing.

September

McLaren was next to find itself in trouble with the sports governing body. The Woking based team was found guilty of running their car with an illegal gearbox. However, the team escaped punishment.

If the Ferraris could have chosen a race in which to occupy the front row of the grid, there was little doubt that the Italian Grand Prix at Monza would have been their number one choice. Jean Alesi picked up the first pole of his career with team-mate Gerhard Berger along side him just over one tenth of a second down in qualifying. Damon Hill would have liked to have started at the head of the grid in the absence of Michael Schumacher who was starting his two race ban, but Hill had to settle for third ahead of the Lotus of Johnny Herbert, which was sixteen places higher on the grid than it was in Belgium thanks to a new lightweight Mugen engine. David Coulthard was fifth in the second Williams ahead of the Ligier of Olivier Panis.

With the world looking on and many willing the Ferrari to victory, Alesi's hopes and those of the fans came to a pit stop halt. On lap 15 of the race, and with a lead of over ten seconds, Alesi came into the pits for a scheduled stop but failed to leave after his car was unable to engage first gear. The disappointment of the *tifosi* was nothing compared with the anger openly expressed by the Frenchman as he stormed into the garage.

A poor pit stop from Berger allowed both Hill and Coulthard to pass the Austrian on the road. Coulthard was to be robbed of second place on the final lap when his Williams died on him, and the fact that he was finally classified sixth for one World Championship point was hardly adequate compensation. Berger's Ferrari and Hakkinen's McLaren finished on the podium behind Hill, with Rubens Barrichello in his Jordan and the second McLaren of Martin Brundle fourth and fifth. Eddie Irvine picked up another one race ban, suspended for three races, for being identified as the culprit of the first corner crash at Monza. Hill had completed the first part of what he hoped would be a *double-wammy*.

Attention turned to Estoril where Ferrari snatched their second successive pole, and their third in five races, as Gerhard Berger pipped Damon Hill by fifteen hundredths of a second in qualifying. But it was the Williams team which was celebrating at the end of the 71 lap race in Portugal with their first one-two of the season putting Damon Hill just one point adrift of the banned Michael Schumacher in the Drivers' World Championship – the 16 points they collected moving them two points clear of Benetton in the race for the Constructors' title.

Coulthard, racing in his last Grand Prix of the season before Nigel Mansell would return for the last three races, showed great promise as he matched Hill for speed, but team orders meant that there was no chance of him actually winning the race. In the end, he finished just six tenths of a second behind Hill, with Hakkinen finishing third for the second race running. Barrichello's Jordan, Verstappen's Benetton and the second McLaren of Martin Brundle took places four, five and six.

In the aftermath Simtek's David Brabham picked up a suspended one race ban for colliding with Jean Alesi's Ferrari at mid-distance, while Ferrari was hit with a $50,000 fine after mechanics kicked down a locked door. The Italian team was also given a one race ban, suspended for three races.

October

The last race in Europe was appropriately the European Grand Prix held at Jerez in Spain. The Championships, both for drivers and constructors, were delicately poised, and the race saw the return of Michael Schumacher from his ban, as well as former World Champion Nigel Mansell after the end of a disappointing season in the Indy Car World Championship. As if to make a point normal service was resumed at the front of the grid with Schumacher ahead of Damon Hill on the front row. Mansell was on the second row beside the Sauber of Heinz-Herald Frentzen, with the consistent Barrichello and Berger in the Ferrari fifth and sixth respectively.

The race itself saw the highest number of finishers in the 1994 season – 19 of the 26 starters reached the chequered flag. Schumacher's strategy of three quick pit stops to Hill's two slower ones, looked likely to cause the German some problems, but the Benetton team's tactics proved to be spot on as Schumacher was able to cruise around for the last few laps allowing Hill to close to half a second as he crossed the line for the final time. Hakkinen picked up four points as he scored a hat-trick of third places, with Irvine, Berger and Frentzen making up the point scorers.

Schumacher's lead over Hill in the Drivers' Championship was now five points, and even if the result of Jerez was repeated at Suzuka, the title race would go to Adelaide with Hill still able to overtake a nine point gap should he win and Schumacher fail to finish in the points. Schumacher's ten points gave Benetton the edge in the Constructors' Championship – Benetton now had a two point advantage over Williams.

November

The conditions on race day at Suzuka were atrocious. Torrential rain had meant that the practice times on Saturday could not be beaten, but most of the drivers, even those who managed to finish the 50 laps, admitted that the race should have been stopped. Johnny Herbert was driving a different car for the third successive race, having switched to Benetton from sister team Ligier.

Attention though was quite rightly focused on the fight for the Drivers' World Championship, with the poor weather on Saturday not allowing Hill a chance to post a time quicker than Schumacher. Pierluigi Martini followed Gianni Morbidelli in crashing out on lap 13 – unlucky for some – but the former had the misfortune to collect a marshal on his way into the barriers. The marshal suffered a broken leg, but thankfully that was the extent of his injuries. The race was immediately red flagged, and after conditions had eased slightly, 37 laps, three less than originally scheduled, were run. Although Schumacher was quicker than Hill on the road, the Williams team had decided to make only one pit stop after the re-start to Benetton's two, and this proved the winning strategy. Hill held off the German to win by three seconds to take both the Drivers' and Constructors' Championships to the last race of the sixteen. Jean Alesi held off Nigel Mansell in a thrilling battle for third place, with Eddie Irvine fifth and Heinz-Harald Frentzen sixth.

The hype leading up to the Adelaide Grand Prix was inevitable if not unbelievable. With less than a week between the rain of Suzuka and the sun of South Australia all teams were faced with a race against time to ensure their cars were in peak condition.

It had been a season of controversy from the start and the finish was no different as Michael Schumacher collided with Damon Hill on lap 35 of the race. Deliberate or not the arguments would rage on, but the incident ensured the Benetton driver his first World Championship.

No one was doubting the fact that the German had been the better driver during the season, but after a year of sadness and controversy, it was a conclusion that the sport could have done without. If Hill had avoided contact with the Benetton and gone on to win the race, then he would have been World Champion, but the reality was that it was his Williams team-mate Nigel Mansell who collected the ten points as Hill collected his thoughts on what might have been.

Schumacher had gone off the track and into a wall, but the momentum of his car meant that he was back on the track as Hill caught up with him. The two cars touched as they both went for the same line into the next corner which resulted in the Benetton being flipped into the air. Schumacher was definitely out of the race, and a broken front suspension meant that Hill's race was also at an end.

Mansell edged out Berger by some two and a half seconds for the final victory of the season, with Martin Brundle, Rubens Barrichello, Olivier Panis and Jean Alesi making up the top six. Mansell's ten points and Benetton's failure to score gave the Constructors' World Championship to Williams by fifteen points, and a controversial season was at a close. Schumacher dedicated his new title to Ayrton Senna, and also apologised to Hill for derogatory remarks he made about the Briton regarding him being an unworthy rival.

Below: Every picture tells a story – Nigel Mansell and newly crowned World Champion Michael Schumacher share a joke. Damon Hill can't see the funny side – and who could blame him.

GP Results '94

At a Glance

GP	Winner	Pole
Brazil	M. Schumacher (Benetton)	A. Senna (Williams)
Pacific	M. Schumacher (Benetton)	A. Senna (Williams)
San Marino	M. Schumacher (Benetton)	A. Senna (Williams)
Monaco	M. Schumacher (Benetton)	M. Schumacher (Benetton)
Spanish	D. Hill (Williams)	M. Schumacher (Benetton)
Canadian	M. Schumacher (Benetton)	M. Schumacher (Benetton)
French	M. Schumacher (Benetton)	D. Hill (Williams)
British	D.Hill (Williams)	D. Hill (Williams)
German	G. Berger (Ferrari)	G. Berger (Ferrari)
Hungarian	M. Schumacher (Benetton)	M. Schumacher (Benetton)
Belgian	D. Hill (Williams)	R. Barrichello (Jordan)
Italian	D. Hill (Williams)	J. Alesi (Ferrari)
Portuguese	D. Hill (Williams)	G. Berger (Ferrari)
European	M. Schumacher (Benetton)	M. Schumacher (Benetton)
Japanese	D. Hill (Williams)	M. Schumacher (Benetton)
Australian	N. Mansell (Williams)	N. Mansell (Williams)

Brazilian – Interlagos, 27 March

Pos	Grid	Driver	Team/Engine	Time/Diff
1	2	M. Schumacher	Benetton Ford	1:35'38.759
2	4	D. Hill	Williams Renault	1 lap down
3	3	J. Alesi	Ferrari	1 lap down
4	14	R. Barrichello	Jordan Hart	1 lap down
5	10	U. Katayama	Tyrrell Yamaha	2 laps down
6	7	K. Wendlinger	Sauber Mercedes	2 laps down
7	21	J. Herbert	Team Lotus Mugen Honda	2 laps down
8	15	P. Martini	Minardi Ford	2 laps down
9	13	E. Comas	Larrousse Ford	3 laps down
10	24	P. Lamy	Team Lotus Mugen Honda	3 laps down
11	19	O. Panis	Ligier Renault	3 laps down
12	26	D. Brabham	Simtek Ford	4 laps down

Failed to Finish

13th – A. Senna (Williams Renault), 55 laps – Spin; 14th – M. Brundle (McLaren Peugeot), 34 laps – Accident; 15th – E. Irvine (Jordan Yamaha), 34 laps– Accident; 16th – J. Verstappen (Benetton Ford), 34 laps – Accident; 17th – E. Bernard (Ligier Renault), 33 laps – Accident; 18th – M. Blundell (Tyrrell Yamaha), 21 laps –

Accident; 19th – C. Fittipaldi (Arrows Ford), 21 laps – Gearbox; 20th – H-H Frentzen (Sauber Mercedes), 15 laps – Spin; 21st – M. Hakkinen (McLaren Peugeot) 13 laps – Electrical; 22nd – M. Alboreto (Minardi Ford), 7 laps – Electrical; 23rd – G. Morbidelli (Arrows Ford), 5 laps – Gearbox; 24th – G. Berger (Ferrari), 5 laps – Air valve leak; 25th – O. Berreta (Larrousse Ford), 2 laps – Accident; 26th – B. Gachot (Pacific Ilmor), 1 lap – Accident.

Pacific – TI Circuit Aida, 17 April

Pos	Grid	Driver	Team/Engine	Time/Diff
1	2	M. Schumacher	Benetton Ford	1:46'01.693
2	5	G. Berger	Ferrari	1'15.300
3	8	R. Barrichello	Jordan Hart	1 lap down
4	9	C. Fittipaldi	Arrows Ford	1 lap down
5	11	H-H Frentzen	Sauber Mercedes	1 lap down
6	16	E. Comas	Larrousse Ford	3 laps down
7	23	J. Herbert	Team Lotus Mugen Honda	3 laps down
8	24	P. Lamy	Team Lotus Mugen Honda	4 laps down
9	22	O. Panis	Ligier Renault	5 laps down
10	18	E. Bernard	Ligier Renault	5 laps down
11	26	R. Ratzenberger	Simtek Ford	5 laps down

Failed to Finish

12th – G. Morbidelli (Arrows Ford), 69 laps – Engine; 13th – K. Wendlinger (Sauber Mercedes), 69 laps – Accident; 14th – M. Alboreto (Minardi Ford), 69 laps – Accident; 15th – M. Brundle (McLaren Peugeot), 67 laps – Engine; 16th – P. Martini (Minardi Ford), 63 laps – Spin; 17th – J. Verstappen (Benetton Ford), 54 laps – Spin; 18th – D. Hill (Williams Renault), 49 laps – Transmission; 19th – A. Suzuki (Jordan Hart), 44 laps – Spin; 20th – U. Katayama (Tyrrell Yamaha), 42 laps – Engine; 21st – M. Hakkinen (McLaren Peugeot), 19 laps – Transmission; 22nd – O. Beretta (Larrousse Ford), 14 laps – Engine; 23rd – D. Brabham (Simtek Ford), 2 laps – Engine; 24th – A. Senna (Williams Renault), 0 laps – Accident; 25th – M. Blundell (Tyrrell Yamaha), 0 laps– Accident; 26th – N. Larini (Ferrari) 0 laps – Accident.

San Marino – Imola, 1 May

Pos	Grid	Driver	Team/Engine	Time/Diff
1	2	M. Schumacher	Benetton Ford	1:28'28.642
2	6	N. Larini	Ferrari	54.942
3	8	M. Hakkinen	McLaren Peugeot	1'10.679
4	10	K. Wendlinger	Sauber Mercedes	1'13.658
5	9	U. Katayama	Tyrrell Yamaha	1 lap down
6	4	D. Hill	Williams Renault	1 lap down
7	7	H-H Frentzen	Sauber Mercedes	1 lap down
8	13	M. Brundle	McLaren Peugeot	1 lap down
9	12	M. Blundell	Tyrrell Yamaha	2 laps down

10	20	J. Herbert	Team Lotus Mugen Honda	2 laps down
11	19	O. Panis	Ligier Renault	2 laps down
12	17	E. Bernard	Ligier Renault	3 laps down
13	16	C. Fittipaldi	Arrows Ford	3 laps down

Failed to Finish

14th – A. de Cesaris (Jordan Hart), 49 laps – Spin; 15th – M. Alboreto (Minardi Ford), 44 laps – Loose wheel; 16th – G. Morbidelli (Arrows Ford), 40 laps – Engine; 17th – P. Martini (Minardi Ford), 37 laps – Spin; 18th – D. Brabham (Simtek Ford), 27 laps – Gearbox; 19th – B. Gachot (Pacific Ilmor), 23 laps – Oil; 20th – O. Beretta (Larrousse Ford), 17 laps – Engine; 21st – G. Berger (Ferrari), 16 laps – Loose wheel; 22nd – A. Senna (Williams Renault) 5 laps – Accident; 23rd – E. Comas (Larrousse Ford), 5 laps – Accident; 24th – JJ Lehto (Benetton Ford), 0 laps – Accident; 25th – P. Lamy (Team Lotus Mugen Honda), 0 laps – Accident.

Monaco – 15 May

Pos	Grid	Driver	Team/Engine	Time/Diff
1	1	M. Schumacher	Benetton Ford	1:49'55.372
2	8	M. Brundle	McLaren Peugeot	37.278
3	3	G. Berger	Ferrari	1'16.824
4	14	A. de Cesaris	Jordan Hart	1 lap down
5	5	J. Alesi	Ferrari	1 lap down
6	2	M. Alboreto	Minardi Ford	1 lap down
7	17	JJ Lehto	Benetton Ford	1 lap down
8	8	O. Beretta	Larrousse Ford	2 laps down
9	20	O. Panis	Ligier Renault	2 laps down
10	13	E. Comas	Larrousse Ford	3 laps down
11	19	P. Lamy	Team Lotus Mugen Honda	5 laps down

Failed to Finish

12th – J. Herbert (Team Lotus Mugen Honda), 68 laps – Gearbox; 13th – P. Belmondo (Pacific Ilmor), 63 laps – Driver fatigue; 14th – B. Gachot (Pacific Ilmor), 49 laps – Gearbox; 15th – C. Fittipaldi (Arrows Ford), 47 laps – Gearbox; 16th – D. Brabham (Simtek Ford), 5 laps – Accident; 17th – M. Blundell (Tyrrell Yamaha),40 laps – Engine; 18th – U. Katayama (Tyrrell Yamaha), 38 laps – Gearbox; 19th – E. Bernard (Ligier Renault), 34 laps – Spin; 20th – R. Barrichello (Jordan Hart), 27 laps – Electrical; 21st – D. Hill (Williams Renault), 0 laps – Accident; 22nd – M. Hakkinen (McLaren Peugeot), 0 laps – Accident; 23rd – G. Morbidelli (Arrows Ford), 0 laps – Accident; 24th – P. Martini (Minardi Ford), 0 laps – Accident.

Spanish – Catalunya, 29 May

Pos	Grid	Driver	Team/Engine	Time/Diff
1	2	D. Hill	Williams Renault	1:36'14.374
2	1	M. Schumacher	Benetton Ford	24.166
3	11	M. Blundell	Tyrrell Yamaha	1'26.969

4	6	J. Alesi	Ferrari	1 lap down
5	18	P. Martini	Minardi Ford	1 lap down
6	13	E. Irvine	Jordan Hart	1 lap down
7	19	O. Panis	Ligier Renault	2 laps down
8	20	E. Bernard	Ligier Renault	3 laps down
9	23	A. Zanardi	Team Lotus Mugen Honda	3 laps down
10	24	D. Brabham	Simtek Ford	4 laps down
11	8	M. Brundle	McLaren Peugeot	6 laps down

Failed to Finish

12th – JJ Lehto (Benetton Ford), 53 laps – Engine; 13th – M. Hakkinen (McLaren Peugeot), 48 laps – Engine; 14th – J. Herbert (Team Lotus Mugen Honda), 41 laps – Spin; 15th – R. Barrichello (Jordan Hart), 39 laps – Engine; 16th – C. Fittipaldi (Arrows Ford), 35 laps – Engine; 17th – D. Coulthard (Williams Renault), 32 laps – Gearbox; 18th – B. Gachot (Pacific Ilmor), 32 laps – Wing damage; 19th – G. Berger (Ferrari), 27 laps – Gearbox; 20th – G. Morbidelli (Arrows Ford), 24 laps – Fuel valve; 21st – H-H Frentzen (Sauber Mercedes), 21 laps – Gearbox; 22nd – E. Comas (Larrousse Ford), 19 laps – Water; 23rd – U. Katayama (Tyrrell Yamaha), 16 laps – Engine; 24th – M. Alboreto (Minardi Ford), 4 laps – Engine; 25th – P. Belmondo (Pacific Ilmor), 3 laps – Spin; 26th – O. Beretta (Larrousse Ford), 0 laps – Engine problem on parade lap.

Canadian – Gilles Villeneuve, 12 June

Pos	Grid	Driver	Team/Engine	Time/Diff
1	1	M. Schumacher	Benetton Ford	1:44'31.887
2	4	D. Hill	Williams Renault	39.660
3	2	J. Alesi	Ferrari	1'13.388
4	3	G. Berger	Ferrari	1'15.609
5	5	D. Coulthard	Williams Renault	1 lap down
6	20	JJ Lehto	Benetton Ford	1 lap down
7	6	R. Barrichello	Jordan Hart	1 lap down
8	17	J. Herbert	Team Lotus Mugen Honda	1 lap down
9	15	P. Martini	Minardi Ford	1 lap down
10	13	M. Blundell	Tyrrell Yamaha	2 laps down
11	18	M. Alboreto	Minardi Ford	2 laps down
11	19	O. Panis	Ligier Renault	3 laps down
14	25	D. Brabham	Simtek Ford	4 laps down

Failed to Finish

15th – A. Zanardi (Team Lotus Mugen Honda), 62 laps – Engine; 16th – M. Hakkinen (McLaren Peugeot), 61 laps – Engine; 17th – O. Beretta (Larrousse Ford), 57 laps – Engine; 18th – G. Morbidelli (Arrows Ford), 50 laps – Gearbox; 19th – B. Gachot (Pacific Ilmor), 47 laps – Oil pressure; 20th – E. Comas (Larrousse Ford), 45 laps – Clutch; 21st – U. Katayama (Tyrrell Yamaha), 44 laps – Spin; 22nd – E. Irvine (Jordan Hart), 40 laps – Spin; 23rd – A. de Cesaris (Sauber Mercedes), 24 laps – Oil leak; 24th – H. H. Frentzen (Sauber Mercedes), 5 laps – Spin; 25th – M. Brundle (McLaren Peugeot), 3 laps – Electrical. **Disqualified:** C. Fittipaldi (Arrows Ford) – Finished sixth but car below minimum weight.

French – Magny-Cours, 3 July

Pos	Grid	Driver	Team/Engine	Time/Diff
1	3	M. Schumacher	Benetton Ford	1:38'35.704
2	1	D. Hill	Williams Renault	12.642
3	5	G. Berger	Ferrari	52.765
4	10	H-H Frentzen	Sauber Mercedes	1 lap down
5	16	P. Martini	Minardi Ford	2 laps down
6	11	A. de Cesaris	Sauber Mercedes	2 laps down
7	19	J. Herbert	Team Lotus Mugen Honda	2 laps down
8	18	C. Fittipaldi	Arrows Ford	2 laps down
9	26	J-M Gounon	Simtek Ford	4 laps down
10	17	M. Blundell	Tyrrell Yamaha	5 laps down

Failed to Finish

11th – E. Comas (Larrousse Ford), 66 laps – Engine; 12th – U. Katayama (Tyrrell Yamaha), 53 laps – Spin; 13th – M. Hakkinen (McLaren Peugeot), 48 laps – Engine; 14th – N.Mansell (Williams Renault), 46 laps – Transmission, 15th – J. Alesi (Ferrari), 41 laps – Accident; 16th – R. Barrichello (Jordan Hart), 41 laps – Accident; 17th – E. Bernard (Ligier Renault), 40 laps – Gearbox; 18th – O. Beretta (Larrousse Ford), 36 laps – Engine; 19th – M. Brundle (McLaren Peugeot), 29 laps – Engine; 20th – G. Morbidelli (Arrows Ford), 28 laps – Accident; 21st – O. Panis (Ligier Renault), 28 laps – (Accident; 22nd – D. Brabham (Simtek Ford), 28 laps – Gearbox; 23rd – J. Verstappen (Benetton Ford), 25 laps – Spin; 24th – E. Irvine (Jordan Hart), 24 laps – Gearbox; 25th – M. Alboreto (Minardi Ford), 21 laps – Engine; 26th – A. Zanardi (Team Lotus Mugen Honda), 19 laps – Engine.

British – Silverstone, 10 July

Pos	Grid	Driver	Team/Engine	Time/Diff
1	1	D. Hill	Williams Renault	1:30'03.640
2	2	M. Schumacher	Benetton Ford	18.778
3	4	J. Alesi	Ferrari	1'08.128
4	5	M. Hakkinen	McLaren Peugeot	1'40.659
5	6	R. Barrichello	Jordan Hart	1'41.751
6	7	D. Coulthard	Williams Renault	1 lap down
7	8	U. Katayama	Tyrrell Yamaha	1 lap down
8	13	H-H Frentzen	Sauber Mercedes	1 lap down
9	10	J. Verstappen	Benetton Ford	1 lap down
10	20	C. Fittipaldi	Arrows Ford	2 laps down
11	14	P. Martini	Minardi Ford	2 laps down
12	21	J. Herbert	Team Lotus Mugen Honda	2 laps down
13	15	O. Panis	Ligier Renault	2 laps down
14	23	E. Bernard	Ligier Renault	2 laps down
15	24	O. Berretta	Larrousse Ford	2 laps down
16	25	D. Brabham	Simtek Ford	3 laps down
17	26	J-M Gounon	Simtek Ford	3 laps down

Failed to Finish

18th – G. Berger (Ferrari), 32 laps – Engine; 19th – M. Blundell (Tyrrell Yamaha), 20 laps – Electrical; 20th – E. Comas (Larrousse Ford), 11 laps – Engine; 21st – A. de Cesaris (Sauber Mercedes), 11 laps – Engine; 22nd – G. Morbidelli (Arrows Ford), 5 laps – Fuel Pump; 23rd – A. Zanardi (Team Lotus Mugen Honda), 4 laps – Engine. **Did not start:** E. Irvine (Jordan Hart) – Engine; M. Brundle (McLaren Peugeot) – Engine.

German – Hockenheim, 31 July

Pos	Grid	Driver	Team/Engine	Time/Diff
1	1	G. Berger	Ferrari	1:22'37.272
2	12	O. Panis	Ligier Renault	54.779
3	14	E. Bernard	Ligier Renault	1'05.042
4	17	C. Fittipaldi	Arrows Ford	1'21.609
5	16	G. Morbidelli	Arrows Ford	1'30.544
6	22	E. Comas	Larrousse Ford	1'45.445
7	24	O. Beretta	Larrousse Ford	1 lap down
8	3	D. Hill	Williams Renault	1 lap down

Failed to Finish

9th – J-M Gounon (Simtek Ford), 39 laps – Engine; 10th – D. Brabham (Simtek Ford), 37 laps – Clutch; 11th – M. Schumacher (Benetton Ford), 20 laps – Engine; 12th – M. Brundle (McLaren Peugeot), 19 laps – Engine; 13th – D. Coulthard (Williams Renault), 17 laps – Electrics; 14th – J. Verstappen (Benetton Ford), 16 laps – Pit fire; 15th – U. Katayama (Tyrrell Yamaha), 6 laps – Throttle; 16th – M. Blundell (Tyrrell Yamaha), 0 laps – Accident; 17th – M. Hakkinen (McLaren Peugeot), 0 laps – Accident; 18th – A. Zanardi (Team Lotus Mugen Honda), 0 laps – Accident; 19th – J. Herbert (Team Lotus Mugen Honda), 0 laps – Accident; 20th – R. Barrichello (Jordan Hart), 0 laps – Accident; 21st – E. Irvine (Jordan Hart), 0 laps – Accident; 22nd – P. Martini (Minardi Ford), 0 laps – Accident; 23rd – M. Alboreto (Minardi Ford), 0 laps – Accident; 24th – J. Alesi (Ferrari), 0 laps – Engine; 25th – A. de Cesaris (Sauber Mercedes), 0 laps – Accident; 26th – H-H Frentzen (Sauber Mercedes), 0 laps – Accident.

Hungarian – Hungaroring, 14 August

Pos	Grid	Driver	Team/Engine	Time/Diff
1	1	M. Schumacher	Benetton Ford	1:48'00.185
2	2	D. Hill	Williams Renault	21.012
3	12	J. Verstappen	Benetton Ford	1'10.329
4	6	M. Brundle	McLaren Peugeot	1 lap down
5	11	M. Blundell	Tyrrell Yamaha	1 lap down
6	9	O. Panis	Ligier Renault	1 lap down
7	20	M. Alboreto	Minardi Ford	2 laps down
8	21	E. Comas	Larrousse Ford	2 laps down
9	25	O. Beretta	Larrousse Ford	2 laps down

10	18	E. Bernard	Ligier Renault	2 laps down
11	23	D. Brabham	Simtek Ford	3 laps down
12	4	G. Berger	Ferrari	4 laps down
13	22	A. Zanardi	Team Lotus Mugen Honda	5 laps down

Failed to Finish

14th – C. Fittipaldi (Arrows Ford), 69 laps – Transmission; 15th – D. Coulthard (Williams Renault), 59 laps – Accident; 16th – J. Alesi (Ferrari), 58 laps – Transmission; 17th – P. Martini (Minardi Ford), 58 laps – Spin; 18th – H-H Frentzen (Sauber Mercedes), 39 laps – Transmission; 19th – J. Herbert (Team Lotus Mugen Honda), 34 laps – Electrical; 20th – A. de Cesaris (Sauber Mercedes), 30 laps – Accident; 21st – G. Morbidelli (Arrows Ford), 30 laps – Accident; 22nd – P. Alliott (McLaren Peugeot), 21 laps – Water leak; 23rd – J-M Gounon (Simtek Ford), 9 laps – Steering; 24th – U. Katayama (Tyrrell Yamaha), 0 laps – Accident; 25th – R. Barrichello (Jordan Hart), 0 laps – Accident; 26th – E. Irvine (Jordan Hart), 0 laps – Accident.

Belgian – Spa-Francorchamps, 28 August

Pos	Grid	Driver	Team/Engine	Time/Diff
1	3	D. Hill	Williams Renault	1:28'47.170
2	8	M. Hakkinen	McLaren Peugeot	51.381
3	6	J. Verstappen	Benetton Ford	1'10.453
4	7	D. Coulthard	Williams Renault	1'45.787
5	12	M. Blundell	Tyrrell Yamaha	1 lap down
6	14	G. Morbidelli	Arrows Ford	1 lap down
7	17	O. Panis	Ligier Renault	1 lap down
8	10	P. Martini	Minardi Ford	1 lap down
9	18	M. Alboreto	Minardi Ford	1 lap down
10	16	E. Bernard	Ligier Renault	2 laps down
11	25	J-M Gounon	Simtek Ford	2 laps down
12	20	J. Herbert	Team Lotus	3 laps down

Failed to Finish

13th – E. Irvine (Jordan Hart), 40 laps – Battery; 14th – C. Fittipaldi (Arrows Ford), 33 laps – Engine; 15th – D. Brabham (Simtek Ford), 29 laps – Wheel came off; 16th – A. de Cesaris (Sauber Mercedes), 27 laps – Throttle; 17th – M. Brundle (McLaren Peugeot), 24 laps – Accident; 18th – R. Barrichello (Jordan Hart), 19 laps – Accident; 19th – U. Katayama (Tyrrell Yamaha), 18 laps – Engine; 20th – P. Adams (Team Lotus Mugen Honda), 15 laps – Accident; 21st – G. Berger (Ferrari), 11 laps – Engine; 22nd – P. Alliott (Larrousse Ford), 11 laps – Engine; 23rd – H-H Frentzen (Sauber Mercedes), 10 laps – Spin; 24th – E. Comas (Larrousse Ford), 3 laps – Engine; 25th – J. Alesi (Ferrari), 2 laps – Engine. **Disqualified:** M. Schumacher (Benetton Ford) – Contravention of technical regulations.

Italian – Monza, 11 September

Pos	Grid	Driver	Team/Engine	Time/Diff
1	3	D. Hill	Williams Renault	1:18'02.754
2	2	G. Berger	Ferrari	4.930
3	7	M. Hakkinen	McLaren Peugeot	25.640
4	16	R. Barrichello	Jordan Hart	50.634
5	15	M. Brundle	McLaren Peugeot	1'25.575
6	5	D. Coulthard	Williams Renault	1 lap down
7	12	E. Bernard	Ligier Renault	1 lap down
8	24	E. Comas	Larrousse Ford	1 lap down
9	20	JJ Lehto	Benetton Ford	1 lap down
10	6	O. Panis	Ligier Renault	1 lap down

Failed to Finish

11th – D. Brabham (Simtek Ford), 46 laps – Brakes; 12th – U. Katayama (Tyrrell Yamaha), 45 laps – Brakes; 13th – C. Fittipaldi (Arrows Ford), 43 laps – Engine; 14th – E. Irvine (Jordan Hart), 41 laps – Engine; 15th – M. Blundell (Tyrrell Yamaha), 39 laps – Brakes; 16th – P. Martini (Minardi Ford), 30 laps – Spin; 17th – M. Alboreto (Minardi Ford), 28 laps – Gearbox; 18th – H-H Frentzen (Sauber Mercedes), 22 laps – Engine; 19th – A. de Cesaris (Sauber Mercedes), 20 laps – Engine; 20th – J-M Gounon (Simtek Ford), 20 laps – Gearbox; 21st – Y. Dalmas (Larrousse Ford), 18 laps – Spin; 22nd – J. Alesi (Ferrari), 14 laps – Transmission; 23rd – J. Herbert (Team Lotus Mugen Honda), 13 laps – Alternator; 24th – J. Verstappen (Benetton Ford), 0 laps – Puncture; 25th – G. Morbidelli (Arrows Ford), 0 laps – Spin; 26th – A. Zanardi (Team Lotus), 0 laps – Puncture.

Portuguese – Estoril, 25 September

Pos	Grid	Driver	Team/Engine	Time/Diff
1	2	D. Hill	Williams Renault	1:41'10.165
2	3	D. Coulthard	Williams Renault	0.603
3	4	M. Hakkinen	McLaren Peugeot	20.193
4	8	R. Barrichello	Jordan Hart	28.003
5	10	J. Verstappen	Benetton Ford	29.385
6	7	M. Brundle	McLaren Peugeot	52.702
7	13	E. Irvine	Jordan Hart	1 lap down
8	11	C. Fittipaldi	Arrows Ford	1 lap down
9	15	O. Panis	Ligier Renault	1 lap down
10	16	G. Morbidelli	Arrows Ford	1 lap down
11	21	E. Bernard	Ligier Renault	1 lap down
12	20	J. Herbert	Team Lotus Mugen Honda	1 lap down
13	18	P. Martini	Minardi Ford	2 laps down
14	19	M. Alboreto	Minardi Ford	2 laps down
15	23	Y. Dalmas	Larrousse Ford	2 laps down
16	26	J-M Gounon	Simtek Ford	4 laps down
17	25	P. Adams	Team Lotus Mugen Honda	4 laps down

Failed to Finish

18th – M. Blundell (Tyrrell Yamaha), 61 laps – Engine; 19th – JJ Lehto (Benetton Ford), 60 laps – Accident; 20th – A. de Cesaris (Sauber Mercedes), 54 laps – Differential; 21st – J. Alesi (Ferrari), 38 laps – Accident; 22nd – D. Brabham (Simtek Ford), 36 laps – Accident; 23rd – H-H Frentzen (Sauber Mercedes), 31 laps – Gearbox; 24th – E. Comas (Larrousse Ford), 27 laps – Suspension; 25th – U. Katayama (Tyrrell Yamaha), 26 laps – Gearbox; 26th – G. Berger (Ferrari), 7 laps – Gearbox.

European – Jerez, 16 October

Pos	Grid	Driver	Team/Engine	Time/Diff
1	1	M. Schumacher	Benetton Ford	1:40'26.689
2	2	D. Hill	Williams Renault	24.689
3	9	M.Hakkinen	McLaren Peugeot	1'09.648
4	10	E. Irvine	Jordan Hart	1'18.466
5	6	G. Berger	Ferrari	1 lap down
6	4	H-H Frentzen	Sauber Mercedes	1 lap down
7	13	U. Katayama	Tyrrell Yamaha	1 lap down
8	7	J. Herbert	Ligier Renault	1 lap down
9	11	O. Panis	Ligier Renault	1 lap down
10	16	J. Alesi	Ferrari	1 lap down
11	8	G. Morbidelli	Arrows Ford	1 lap down
12	5	R. Barrichello	Jordan Hart	1 lap down
13	14	M. Blundell	Tyrrell Yamaha	1 lap down
14	20	M. Alboreto	Minardi Ford	2 laps down
15	17	P. Martini	Minardi Ford	2 laps down
16	21	A. Zanardi	Team Lotus Mugen Honda	2 laps down
17	19	C. Fittipaldi	Arrows Ford	3 laps down
18	22	E. Bernard	Team Lotus Mugen Honda	3 laps down
19	26	D. Schiattarella	Simtek Ford	5 laps down

Failed to Finish

20th – N. Mansell (Williams Renault), 47 laps – Spin; 21st – D. Brabham (Simtek Ford), 43 laps – Engine; 22nd – A. de Cesaris (Sauber Mercedes), 37 laps – Throttle; 23rd – E. Comas (Larrousse Ford), 37 laps – Electrical; 24th – J. Verstappen (Benetton Ford), 15 laps – Spin; 25th – H. Noda (Larrousse Ford), 10 laps – Electrical; 26th – M. Brundle (McLaren Peugeot), 8 laps – Engine.

Japanese – Suzuka, 6 November

Pos	Grid	Driver	Team/Engine	Time/Diff
1	2	D. Hill	Williams Renault	1:55'53.530
2	1	M. Schumacher	Benetton Ford	3.365
3	7	J. Alesi	Ferrari	52.045
4	4	N. Mansell	Williams Renault	56.074
5	6	E. Irvine	Jordan Hart	1'42.107

6	3	H-H Frentzen	Sauber Mercedes	1'59.863
7	8	M. Hakkinen	McLaren Peugeot	2'02.958
8	18	C. Fittipaldi	Arrows Ford	1 lap down
9	22	E. Comas	Larrousse Ford	1 lap down
10	25	M. Salo	Team Lotus Mugen Honda	1 lap down
11	19	O. Panis	Ligier Renault	1 lap down
12	24	D. Brabham	Simtek Ford	2 laps down
13	17	A. Zanardi	Team Lotus Mugen Honda	2 laps down

Failed to Finish

14th – M. Blundell (Tyrrell Yamaha), 26 laps – Spin; 15th – R. Barrichello (Jordan Yamaha), 16 laps – Electrical; 16th – M. Brundle (McLaren Peugeot), 13 laps – Spin; 17th – G. Morbidelli (Arrows Ford), 13 laps – Spin; 18th – G. Berger (Ferrari), 10 laps – Electrical; 19th – P. Martini (Minardi Ford), 10 laps – Spin; 20th – M. Alboreto (Minardi Ford), 10 laps – Spin; 21st – F. Lagorce (Ligier Renault), 10 laps – Spin; 22nd – U. Katayama (Tyrrell Yamaha), 3 laps – Spin; 23rd – J. Herbert (Benetton Ford), 3 laps – Spin; 24th – T. Inoue (Simtek Ford), 3 laps – Spin; 25th – H. Noda (Larrousse Ford), 0 laps – Spin; 26th – JJ Lehto (Sauber Mercedes), 0 laps – Spin.

Australian – Adelaide, 13 November

Pos	Grid	Driver	Team/Engine	Time/Diff
1	1	N. Mansell	Williams Renault	1:47'51.480
2	11	G. Berger	Ferrari	2.511
3	9	M. Brundle	McLaren Peugeot	52.487
4	5	R. Barrichello	Jordan Hart	1'10.530
5	12	O. Panis	Ligier Renault	1 lap down
6	8	J. Alesi	Ferrari	1 lap down
7	10	H-H Frentzen	Sauber Mercedes	1 lap down
8	19	C. Fittipaldi	Arrows	1 lap down
9	18	P. Martini	Minardi Ford	2 laps down
10	17	JJ Lehto	Sauber Mercedes	2 laps down
11	20	F. Lagorce	Ligier Renault	2 laps down
12		M. Hakkinen	McLaren Peugeot	5 laps down

Failed to Finish

13th –M. Alboreto (Minardi Ford), 69 laps – Suspension; 14th – M. Blundell (Tyrrell Yamaha), 66 laps – Accident; 15th – J-D Deletraz (Larrousse Ford), 56 laps – Gearbox; 16th – M. Salo (Team Lotus Mugen Honda), 49 laps – Electrics; 17th – D. Brabham (Simtek Ford), 49 laps – Engine; 18th – A. Zanardi (Team Lotus Mugen Honda), 40 laps – Throttle cable; 19th – M. Schumacher (Benetton Ford), 35 laps – Accident; 20th – D. Hill (Williams Renault), 35 laps – Wishbone; 21st – D. Schiattarella (Simtek Ford), 21 laps – Gearbox; 22nd – U. Katayama (Tyrrell Yamaha), 19 laps – Spin; 23rd – H. Noda (Larrousse Ford), 18 laps – Oil leak; 24th – G. Morbidelli (Arrows Ford), 17 laps – Oil pump; 25th – E Irvine (Jordan Hart),15 laps – Spin/fire; 26th – J. Herbert (Benetton Ford) 13 laps – Gearbox.

Driver	Team	B	P	S	M	E	C	F	B	G	H	B	I	P	E	J	A	Pts
M. Schumacher	Benetton	1f	1f	R	1pf	2pf	1pf	1	1pf	1p	1pf	1f	1f	1	1pf	2p	Rf	92
D. Hill	Williams	2	2	6f	R	R	4	2pf	D	R	2	2f	2	1	2	1f	Rf	91
G. Berger	Ferrari	R	R	R	3	R	R	3	1pf	1p	12	R	3	Rp	5	R	12*	41
M. Hakkinen	McLaren	R	2	3	R	R	R	R	3	R	R	R	2	3	R	7	6	26
J. Alesi	Ferrari	3	R	—	5	4	3	R	R	R	—	2	Rp	3	10	3	—	24
R. Barrichello	Jordan	4	3	FS	R	3	7	R	4	R	R	Rp	4	4	12	R	4	19
M. Brundle	McLaren	—	R	8	2	11*	5	R	5	Rf	4*	4	5	6	R	R	3	16
D. Coulthard	Williams	—	—	—	—	5	—	5	R	—	—	—	6*	2f	R	4	—	14
N. Mansell	Williams	—	—	—	—	—	—	R	—	—	—	—	—	Rp	R	R	1p	13
J. Verstappen	Benetton	R	R	—	—	7	12	R	5	R	3	R	—	—	9	11	R	10
O. Panis	Ligier	11	9	11	9	R	12	9	8	2	6	5	10	D	13	11	5	9
M. Blundell	Tyrrell	R	R	9	FS	3	10	10	—	7	5	R	R	D	R	R	6	8
H-H. Frentzen	Sauber	R	5	7	2	R	R	4	7	R	5	7	R	6	6	R	7	7
N. Larini	Ferrari	—	R	2	—	—	—	—	—	—	—	—	—	—	—	—	—	6
C. Fittipaldi	Arrows	R	4	13*	R	R	D	8	9	4	14	R	8	8	17	8	8	6
E. Irvine	Jordan	—	R	—	6	6	R	R	R	13	R	6	13	7	4	5	R	6
U. Katayama	Tyrrell	5	R	5	R	R	R	6	6	R	10	R	7	7	7	R	R	5
E. Bernard	Ligier	R	10	12	R	8	13	R	13	3	10	R	R	10	18	—	—	—
	Lotus	—	—	—	—	—	—	—	—	—	—	—	—	—	—	—	—	4
K. Wendlinger	Sauber	6	R	4	FS	—	—	—	—	—	—	—	—	—	—	—	—	4
A. de Cesaris	Jordan	—	R	—	4	—	—	—	—	—	—	—	—	—	—	—	—	4
	Sauber	—	—	—	—	R	R	R	R	R	R	R	R	R	9	R	R	
P. Martini	Minardi	8	R	R	R	9	5	R	10	R	8	8	12	15	R	9	R	4
G. Morbidelli	Arrows	R	R	R	R	R	R	R	R	R	6	R	R	9	11	R	R	3

Driver	Team	B	P	S	M	E	C	F	B	G	H	B	I	P	E	J	A	Pts
E. Comas	Larrousse	9	6	R	10	R	R	R	R	6	8	R	8	13	14	9	—	2
M. Alboreto	Minardi	R	R	R	6	R	R	R	R	7	7	9	9	R	—	—	R	1
JJ Lehto	Benetton	—	—	R	7	R	R	R	R	R	R	R	R	R	8	R	R	1
	Sauber	—	—	—	—	—	—	—	—	—	—	—	—	—	—	—	—	—
P. Adams	Lotus	—	—	—	—	—	—	—	—	—	—	16	—	R	—	—	—	0
P. Alliot	McLaren	—	—	—	—	—	—	R	—	—	—	—	—	—	—	—	—	0
	Larrousse	—	—	—	—	—	—	—	—	—	—	—	—	—	—	—	—	—
P. Belmondo	Pacific	FQ	FQ	FQ	R	R	FQ	FQ	FQ	FQ	R	FQ	—	—	—	—	—	0
O. Beretta	Larrousse	R	R	R	8	10	14	9	14	7	R	11	11	15	—	R	R	0
D. Brabham	Simtek	12	R	R	R	R	15	R	R	R	R	12	R	14	R	R	13	0
Y. Dalmas	Larrousse	—	—	—	—	R	—	R	—	—	—	—	14	R	—	R	R	0
J-D Deletraz	Larrousse	—	—	—	—	—	—	—	—	—	—	—	R	R	—	R	—	0
B. Gachot	Pacific	R	FQ	R	R	R	R	FQ	FQ	FQ	R	R	—	—	—	—	—	0
J-M Gounon	Simtek	—	—	—	—	—	—	7	R	R	R	11	R	15	8	—	—	0
J. Herbert	Lotus	7	7	10	R	R	8	9	7	11	R	11	—	10	R	R	R	0
	Benetton	—	—	—	—	—	—	—	—	—	—	—	—	—	—	—	—	—
T. Inoue	Simtek	—	—	—	—	FS	—	—	—	—	—	—	—	—	—	R	R	0
F. Lagorce	Ligier	—	—	—	—	—	—	—	—	—	—	—	—	—	R	R	11	0
P. Lamy	Lotus	10	8	R	11	—	—	—	—	—	—	—	—	—	—	—	—	0
A. Montermini	Simtek	—	—	—	—	FS	—	—	—	—	—	—	—	—	R	—	R	0
H. Noda	Larrousse	—	—	—	—	—	—	—	—	—	—	—	—	—	R	R	R	0
R. Ratzenberger	Simtek	FQ	11	FS	—	—	—	—	—	—	—	—	—	—	—	—	—	0
M. Salo	Lotus	—	—	—	—	—	—	—	—	—	—	—	—	—	19	10	R	0
D. Schiattarella	Simtek	Rp	Rp	—	—	—	—	—	—	—	—	—	—	—	—	—	R	0
A. Senna	Williams	R	R	R	—	—	—	—	—	—	—	—	—	—	—	—	—	0
A. Suzuki	Jordan	—	R	—	—	—	—	—	—	—	—	—	—	—	16	13	R	0
A. Zanardi	Lotus	—	—	15	9	—	—	—	—	—	13	—	R	—	—	—	—	0

*= classified but not running at finish. D=Disqualified. FS=Failed to Start. FQ=Failed to Qualify.
p=pole position. f=fastest lap

FIA DRIVERS' CHAMPIONSHIP PLACINGS 1994

Pos	Driver	Team	Points
1st	Michael Schumacher (Germany)	Benetton	92
2nd	Damon Hill (GB)	Williams	91
3rd	Gerhard Berger (Austria)	Ferrari	41
4th	Mika Hakkinen (Finland)	McLaren	26
5th	Jean Alesi (France)	Ferrari	24
6th	Rubens Barrichello (Brazil)	Jordan	19
7th	Martin Brundle (GB)	McLaren	16
8th	David Coulthard (GB)	Williams	14
9th	Nigel Mansell (GB)	Williams	13
10th	Jos Verstappen (Holland)	Benetton	10
11th	Olivier Panis (France)	Ligier	9
12th	Mark Blundell (GB)	Tyrrell	8
13th	Heinz-Harald Frentzen (Germany)	Sauber	7
14th	Nicola Larini (Italy)	Ferrari	6
=	Christian Fittipaldi (Brazil)	Arrows	6
=	Eddie Irvine (GB)	Jordan	6
17th	Ukyo Katayama (Japan)	Tyrrell	5
18th	Karl Wendlinger (Austria)	Sauber	4
=	Andrea de Cesaris (Italy)	Jordan/Sauber	4
=	Pierluigi Martini (Italy)	Minardi	4
=	Eric Bernard (France)	Ligier	4
22nd	Gianni Morbidelli (Italy)	Arrows	3
23rd	Erik Comas (France)	Larrousse	2
24th	Michele Alboreto (Italy)	Minardi	1
=	JJ Lehto (Finland)	Benetton	1

CONSTRUCTORS' CHAMPIONSHIP PLACINGS 1994

Pos	Team	Points
1st	Williams	118
2nd	Benetton	103
3rd	Ferrari	71
4th	McLaren	42
5th	Jordan	28
6th	Ligier	13
=	Tyrrell	13
8th	Sauber	12
9th	Arrows	9
10th	Minardi	5
11th	Larrousse	2

DRIVERS' WORLD CHAMPIONSHIP WINNERS 1950-1994

R=Races, W=Wins, P=Poles, F=Fastest laps

Year	Driver	Age	Country	Car	R	W	P	F
1950	Giuseppe Farina	44	Italy	Alfa Romeo	7	3	2	3
1951	Juan-Manuel Fangio	40	Argentina	Alfa Romeo	8	3	4	5
1952	Alberto Ascari	34	Italy	Ferrari	8	6	5	5
1953	Alberto Ascari	35	Italy	Ferrari	9	5	6	4
1954	Juan-Manuel Fangio	43	Argentina	Merc/Maserati	9	6	5	3
1955	Juan-Manuel Fangio	44	Argentina	Mercedes	7	4	3	3
1956	Juan-Manuel Fangio	45	Argentina	Lancia/Ferrari	8	3	5	3
1957	Juan-Manuel Fangio	46	Argentina	Maserati	8	4	4	2
1958	Mike Hawthorn	29	G. Britain	Ferrari	11	1	4	5
1959	Jack Brabham	33	Australia	Cooper	9	2	1	1
1960	Jack Brabham	34	Australia	Cooper	10	5	3	3
1961	Phil Hill	34	USA	Ferrari	8	2	5	2
1962	Graham Hill	33	G. Britain	BRM	9	4	1	3
1963	Jim Clark	27	G. Britain	Lotus	10	7	7	6
1964	John Surtees	30	G. Britain	Ferrari	10	2	2	2
1965	Jim Clark	29	G. Britain	Lotus	10	6	6	6
1966	Jack Brabham	40	Australia	Brabham	9	4	3	1
1967	Denis Hulme	31	N. Zealand	Brabham	11	2	0	2
1968	Graham Hill	39	G. Britain	Lotus	12	3	2	0
1969	Jackie Stewart	30	G. Britain	Matra	11	6	2	5
1970	Jochen Rindt	28	Austria	Lotus	13	5	3	1
1971	Jackie Stewart	32	G. Britain	Tyrrell	11	6	6	3
1972	Emerson Fittipaldi	26	Brazil	Lotus	12	5	3	1
1973	Jackie Stewart	34	Brazil	Tyrrell	15	5	3	1
1974	Emerson Fittipaldi	28	Brazil	McLaren	15	3	2	0
1975	Niki Lauda	26	Austria	Ferrari	14	5	9	2
1976	James Hunt	29	G. Britain	McLaren	16	6	8	2
1977	Niki Lauda	28	Austria	Ferrari	17	3	2	3
1978	Mario Andretti	38	USA	Lotus	16	6	8	3
1979	Jody Scheckter	29	USA	Ferrari	15	3	1	1
1980	Alan Jones	34	Australia	Williams	14	5	3	5
1981	Nelson Piquet	29	Brazil	Brabham	15	3	4	1
1982	Keke Rosberg	34	Finland	Williams	16	1	1	0
1983	Nelson Piquet	31	Brazil	Brabham	15	3	1	4
1984	Niki Lauda	35	Australia	McLaren	16	5	0	5
1985	Alain Prost	30	France	McLaren	16	5	2	5
1986	Alain Prost	31	France	McLaren	16	4	1	2
1987	Nelson Piquet	35	Brazil	Williams	16	3	4	4
1988	Ayrton Senna	28	Brazil	McLaren	16	8	13	3
1989	Alain Prost	34	France	McLaren	16	4	2	5
1990	Ayrton Senna	30	Brazil	McLaren	16	6	10	2

1991	Ayrton Senna	31	Brazil	McLaren	16	7	8	2
1992	Nigel Mansell	39	G. Britain	Williams	16	9	14	8
1993	Alain Prost	38	France	Williams	16	7	13	6
1994	Michael Schumacher	25	Germany	Benetton	16	8	6	8

DRIVERS' WORLD CHAMPIONSHIP WINS BY NUMBER

Titles	Driver	Country	Year
5	Juan-Manuel Fangio	Argentina	1951, 1954, 1955, 1956 & 1957
4	Alain Prost	France	1985, 1986, 1989 & 1993
3	Jack Brabham	Australia	1959, 1960 & 1966
3	Jackie Stewart	Great Britain	1969, 1971 & 1973
3	Niki Lauda	Austria	1975, 1977 & 1984
3	Nelson Piquet	Brazil	1981, 1983 & 1987
3	Ayrton Senna	Brazil	1988, 1990 & 1991
2	Alberto Ascari	Italy	1952 & 1953
2	Graham Hill	Great Britain	1962 & 1968
2	Jim Clark	Great Britain	1963 & 1965
2	Emerson Fittipaldi	Brazil	1972 & 1974
1	Giuseppe Farina	Italy	1950
1	Mike Hawthorn	Great Britain	1958
1	Phil Hill	USA	1961
1	John Surtees	Great Britain	1964
1	Denis Hulme	New Zealand	1967
1	Jochen Rindt	Austria	1970
1	James Hunt	Great Britain	1976
1	Mario Andretti	USA	1978
1	Jody Scheckter	USA	1979
1	Alan Jones	Australia	1980
1	Keke Rosberg	Finland	1982
1	Nigel Mansell	Great Britain	1992
1	Michael Schumacher	Germany	1994

1994 DRIVERS ALL-TIME RECORDS

Driver	No	WC	1st	2nd	3rd	4th	5th	6th	P	FL	TP
Philippe Adams	2	—									—
Michele Alboreto	194	—	5	9	9	10	8	6*	2	5	186.5
Jean Alesi	85	—		4	9	9	5	3	1	1	100
Philippe Alliot	109	—				1	5	—			7
Rubens Barrichello	31	—		1	5	1	—	1	—		21
Paul Belmondo	7	—									—
Olivier Beretta	10	—									—
Gerhard Berger	163	—	9	15	14	18	8	8	10	16	307

Driver	No	WC	1st	2nd	3rd	4th	5th	6th	P	FL	TP
Eric Bernard	45	—	—	—	1	1	—	3	—	—	10
Mark Blundell	46	—	—	3	—	3	1	—	—	—	19
David Brabham	24	—	—	—	—	—	—	—	—	—	—
Martin Brundle	131	—	—	2	6	6	11	7	—	—	83
Andrea de Cesaris	208	—	—	2	3	7	4	6	1	1	59
Erik Comas	59	—	—	—	—	—	1	5	—	—	7
David Coulthard	8	—	—	1	—	1	2	1	—	2	14
Yannick Dalmas	23	—	—	—	—	—	1	—	—	—	2
Jean-Denis Deletraz	1	—	—	—	—	—	1	—	—	—	—
Pedro Diniz	—	—	—	—	—	—	—	—	—	—	—
Christian Fittipaldi	40	—	—	—	—	3	1	1	—	—	12
H-H Frentzen	15	—	—	—	—	1	1	2	—	—	7
Bertrand Gachot	36	—	—	—	—	—	1	3	—	1	5
Jean-Marc Gounon	9	—	—	—	—	—	—	—	—	—	—
Mika Hakkinen	48	—	—	1	6	2	2	3	—	—	43
Johnny Herbert	63	—	—	—	—	4	2	2	—	—	18
Damon Hill	34	—	9	9	3	1	—	1	4	10	160
Taki Inoue	1	—	—	—	—	—	—	—	—	—	—
Eddie Irvine	15	—	—	—	—	1	1	2	—	—	7
Ukyo Katayama	46	—	—	—	—	—	2	1	—	—	5
Franck Lagorce	2	—	—	—	—	—	—	—	—	—	—
Pedro Lamy	8	—	—	—	—	—	—	—	—	—	—
Nicola Larini	44	—	—	1	—	—	—	—	—	—	6
JJ Lehto	62	—	—	—	1	1	1	1	—	—	10
Nigel Mansell	185	1	31	17	11	8	6	9	32	30	482
Pierluigi Martini	110	—	—	—	—	2	4	4	—	—	18
Andrea Montermini		—	—	—	—	—	—	—	—	—	—
Gianni Morbidelli	50	—	—	—	—	—	1	2*	—	—	3.5
Hideki Noda	3	—	—	—	—	—	—	—	—	—	—
Olivier Panis	16	—	—	1	—	—	1	1	—	—	9
Roland Ratzenberger	1	—	—	—	—	—	—	—	—	—	—
Mika Salo	2	—	—	—	—	—	—	—	—	—	—
Mimmo Schiattarella	2	—	—	—	—	—	—	—	—	—	—
Michael Schumacher	52	1	10	10	7	3	1	2	6	15	201
Ayrton Senna	161	3	41	23	16	7	6	3	65	19	614
Aguri Suzuki	59	—	—	—	—	1	—	3	—	—	7
Jos Verstappen	10	—	—	—	2	—	1	—	—	—	10
Karl Wendlinger	35	—	—	—	—	3	1	3	—	—	14
Alessandro Zanardi	25	—	—	—	—	—	—	1	—	—	1

No=Number of Grand Prixs. WC=Number of World Championship titles. 1st, 2nd etc= Number of times finished in this position. P=Number of Poles. FL=Number of Fastest Laps. TP=Total number of World Championship Points won to date.
* includes 0.5. for 6th place in race that was stopped.

WORLD CHAMPIONSHIP LAST RACE DECIDERS

Year	Grand Prix	Circuit	Drivers
1950	Italian	Monza	Farina (30), Fangio (27), Fagioli (24)
1951	Spanish	Pedralbes	Fangio (31),Ascari (25)
1956	Italian	Monza	Fangio (30), Collins (25)*
1958	Morocco	Casablanca	Hawthorn (42), Moss (41)
1959	USA	Sebring	Brabham (31), Brooks (27), Moss (25.5)
1962	S. African	E. London	G. Hill (42), Clark (30)
1964	Mexican	Mexico City	Surtees (40), G. Hill (39), Clark (32)
1967	Mexican	Mexico City	Hulme (51), Brabham (46)
1968	Mexican	Mexico City	G. Hill (48), Stewart (36), Hulme (33)
1974	USA	Watkins Glen	E. Fittipaldi (55), Regazzoni (52), Scheckter (45)
1976	Japanesse	Mount Fuji	Hunt (69), Lauda (68)
1981	USA	Las Vegas	Piquet (50), Reutemann (49), Laffite (46)
1982	USA	Las Vegas	Rosberg (44), Watson (39)†
1983	S.African	Kyalami	Piquet (59), Prost (57), Arnoux (49)
1984	Portuguese	Estoril	Lauda (72), Prost (71.5)
1986	Australian	Adelaide	Prost (72), Mansell (70), Piquet (69)
1994	Australian	Adelaide	Schumacher (92), D. Hill (91)

Finished third in championship after Moss † *Finished joint second with Prioni Numbers in brackets are final points total.*

WORLD CHAMPIONSHIP DRIVERS WITH 100 POINTS OR MORE

Driver	Points	Driver	Points	Driver	Points
Prost	768.5	Fangio	245	D. Hill	160
Senna	610	Laffite	228	Rosberg	159.5
Piquet	481.5	Regazzoni	209	Depailler	139
Mansell	480	Schumacher	201	Ascari	107.5
Lauda	420.5	Jones	199	Gurney	133
Stewart	359	Peterson	206	Boutsen	132
Berger	307	McLaren	188.5	Farina	116.3
Reutemann	298	Moss	186.5	Hawthorn	112.5
G. Hill	270	Alboreto	185.5	De Angelis	122
E. Fittipaldi	281	Arnoux	181	Rindt	107
Patrese	281	Ickx	181	Ginther	107
Clark	255	Andretti	180	Villeneuve	101
J. Brabham	253	Surtees	180	Tambay	103
Scheckter	246	Hunt	179	Pironi	101
Hulme	248	Watson	169	Alesi	100

DRIVERS WITH FIVE OR MORE GRAND PRIX WINS

Wins	Driver
51	Alain Prost (France)
41	Ayrton Senna (Brazil)
31	Nigel Mansell (Great Britain)
27	Jackie Stewart (Great Britain)
25	Jim Clark (Great Britain) & Niki Lauda (Austria)
24	Juan-Manuel Fangio (Italy)
23	Nelson Piquet (Brazil)
16	Stirling Moss (Great Britain)
14	Jack Brabham (Australia), Emerson Fittipaldi (Brazil) & Graham Hill (Great Britain)
13	Alberto Ascari (Italy)
12	Mario Andretti (USA), Alan Jones (Australia) & Carlos Reutemann (Argentina)
10	James Hunt (Great Britain), Ronnie Peterson (Switzerland), Jody Scheckter (USA) & Michael Schumacher (Germany)
9	Gerhard Berger (Austria) & Damon Hill (Great Britain)
8	Denis Hulme (New Zealand) & Jacky Ickx (Belgium)
7	Rene Arnoux (France)
6	Tony Brooks (Great Britain), Jacques Laffite (France), Riccardo Patrese (Italy), Jochen Rindt (Austria), John Surtees (Great Britain) & Gilles Villeneuve (Canada)
5	Michele Alboreto (Italy), Giuseppe Farina (Italy), Clay Regazzoni (Switzerland), Keke Rosberg (Finland) & John Watson (Great Britain)

DRIVERS WITH FIVE OR MORE POLE POSITIONS

Poles	Driver
65	Ayrton Senna (Brazil)
33	Jim Clark (Great Britain) & Alain Prost (France)
32	Nigel Mansell (Great Britain)
28	Juan-Manuel Fangio (Italy)
24	Niki Lauda (Austria) & Nelson Piquet (Brazil)
18	Mario Andretti (USA) & Rene Arnoux (France)
17	Jackie Stewart (Great Britain)
16	Stirling Moss (Great Britain)
14	Giuseppe Farina (Italy), James Hunt (Great Britain) & Ronnie Peterson (Switzerland)
13	Jack Brabham (Australia), Graham Hill (Great Britain), Jacky Ickx (Belgium)

10	Gerhard Berger (Austria) & Jochen Rindt (Austria)
8	Riccardo Patrese (Italy) & John Surtees (Great Britain)
7	Jacques Laffite (France)
6	Emerson Fittipaldi (Brazil), Phil Hill (USA), Jean-Pierre Labouille (France), Alan Jones (Australia), Carlos Reutemann (Argentina) & Michael Schumacher (Germany)
5	Chris Amon (New Zealand), Giuseppe Farina (Italy), Clay Regazzoni (Switzerland), Keke Rosberg (Finland) & Patrick Tambay (France)

DRIVERS WITH FIVE OR MORE FASTEST LAPS

No	Driver
41	Alain Prost (France)
30	Nigel Mansell (Great Britain)
28	Jim Clark (Great Britain)
25	Niki Lauda (Austria)
23	Juan-Manuel Fangio (Italy) & Nelson Piquet (Brazil)
20	Stirling Moss (Great Britain)
19	Ayton Senna (Brazil)
16	Gerhard Berger (Austria)
15	Clay Regazzoni (Switzerland), Michael Schumacher (Germany) & Jackie Stewart (Great Britain)
14	Jacky Ickx (Belgium)
13	Alan Jones (Australia) & Riccardo Patrese (Italy)
12	Rene Arnoux (France)
11	Alberto Ascari (Italy) & John Surtees (Great Britain)
10	Mario Andretti (USA), Jack Brabham (Australia), Damon Hill (Great Britain) & Graham Hill (Great Britain)
9	Denis Hulme (New Zealand) & Ronnie Peterson (USA)
8	James Hunt (Great Britain)
7	Jacques Laffite (France) & Gilles Villeneuve (Canada)
6	Giuseppe Farina (Italy), Jose Gonzalez (Argentina), Dan Gurney (USA), Mike Hawthorn (Great Britain), Phil Hill (USA), Didier Pironi (France) & Jody Scheckter (USA)
5	Carlos Pace (Brazil) & John Watson (Great Britain)

DRIVERS WHO HAVE COMPLETED 100 GRAND PRIX OR MORE

No	Driver
256	Riccardo Patrese (Italy)
208	Andrea de Cesaris (Italy)
204	Nelson Piquet (Brazil)
199	Alain Prost (France)
194	Michele Alboreto (Italy)
185	Nigel Mansell (Great Britain)
176	Graham Hill (Great Britain) & Jacques Laffite (France)
171	Niki Lauda (Austria)
163	Gerhard Berger (Austria) & Thierry Boutsen (Bel)
161	Ayrton Senna (Brazil)
152	John Watson (Great Britain)
149	Rene Arnoux (France)
147	Derek Warwick (Great Britain)
146	Carlos Reutemann (Argentina)
144	Emerson Fittipaldi (Brazil)
135	Jean-Pierre Jarier (France)
132	Eddie Cheever (USA) & Clay Regazzoni (Switzerland)
131	Martin Brundle (Great Britain)
128	Mario Andretti (USA)
126	Jack Brabham (Australia)
123	Ronnie Peterson (USA)
116	Jacky Ickx (Belgium) & Alan Jones (Austria)
114	Keke Rosberg (Finland) & Patrick Tambay (France)
112	Denis Hulme (New Zealand) & Jody Scheckter (USA)
111	John Surtees (Great Britain)
110	Pierluigi Martini (Italy)
109	Philippe Alliot (France)
108	Elio de Angelis (Italy)
105	Jochen Mass (Germany)
102	Joakim Bonnier (Switzerland)
101	Bruce McLaren (New Zealand)
100	–

DRIVERS WITH MORE THAN 5 POLE POSITIONS IN A SEASON

Poles	Races	Driver	Year(s)
14	16	Mansell	1992
13	16/16	Senna	1988 and 1989
	16	Prost	1993
10	16	Senna	1990

9	15/14	Lauda	1974 and 1975
	15	Peterson	1973
	16	Piquet	1984
8	16/16	Senna	1986 and 1991
	16	Hunt	1976
	16	Andretti	1978
	16	Mansell	1987
7	10	Clark	1963
	17	Andretti	1977
	16	Senna	1985
6	9/10/11	Clark	1962, 1965 and 1967
	9	Ascari	1953
	11	Stewart	1971
	17	Hunt	1977
	16	Schumacher	1994

DRIVERS WITH 3 OR MORE SUCCESSIVE GRAND PRIX WINS

Wins	Driver	Year	Grand Prix
9	Ascari	1952/53	Bel, Fra, GB, Ger, Hol, Ita/Arg, Hol, Bel
5	Brabham	1960	Hol, Bel, Fra, GB, Por
	Clark	1965	Bel, Fra, GB, Hol, Ger
	Mansell	1992	SA, Mex, Bra, Esp, San
4	Senna	1988	GB, Ger, Hon, Bel
		1991	USA, Bra, San, Mon
	Fangio	1953/54	Ita/Arg, Bel, Fra
	Clark	1963	Bel, Hol, Fra, GB
	Brabham	1966	Fra, GB, Hol, Ger
	Rindt	1970	Hol, Fra, GB, Ger
	Prost	1993	Can, Fra, GB, Ger
	Schumacher	1994	Bra, Pac, San, Mon
3	Fangio	1954	Ger, Sui, Ita
		1957	Arg, Mon, Fra
	Stewart	1969	Hol, Fra, GB
		1971	Fra, GB, Ger
	Lauda	1975	Mon, Bel, Sue
		1975/76	USA/Bra, SA
	Jones	1979	Ger, Aut, Hol
		1980/81	Can, USAE/USAW
	Prost	1984/85	Eur, Por/Bra
		1990	Mex, Fra, GB
	Mansell	1991	Fra, GB, Ger
		1992	Fra, GB, Ger
	Moss	1957/58	Pes, Ita/Arg
	Clark	1967/68	USA, Mex/SA

	Senna	1989	San, Mon, Mex
	D. Hill	1993	Hon, Bel, Ita
		1994	Bel, Ita, Por

DRIVERS TO WIN THEIR NATIONAL GRAND PRIX

Wins	Driver	Nat	Year(s)
6	Prost	French	1981, 1983, 1988, 1989, 1990, 1993
5	Clark	British	1962, 1963, 1964, 1965, 1967
4	Fangio	Argentine	1954, 1955, 1956, 1957
	Mansell	British	1986, 1987, 1991, 1992
2	Ascari	Italian	1951, 1952
	Moss	British	1955, 1957
	Stewart	British	1969, 1971
	E. Fittipaldi	Brazilian	1973, 1974
	Piquet	Brazilian	1983, 1986
	Senna	Brazilian	1991, 1993
1	Farina	Italian	1950
	Collins	British	1958
	Scarfiotti	Italian	1966
	Pace	Brazilian	1975
	Scheckter	S. African	1975
	Andretti	American	1977
	Hunt	British	1977
	Villeneuve	Canadian	1978
	Jabouille	French	1979
	Watson	British	1981
	Arnoux	French	1982
	Lauda	Austrian	1984
	D. Hill	British	1994

CONSTRUCTORS' WORLD CHAMPIONSHIPS PER TYPE

Titles	Car	Year(s)
8	Ferrari	1961, 1964, 1975, 1976, 1977, 1979, 1982, 1983
7	Lotus	1963, 1965, 1968, 1970, 1972, 1973 & 1978
7	McLaren	1974, 1984, 1985, 1988, 1989, 1990 & 1991
7	Williams	1980, 1981, 1986, 1987, 1992, 1993 & 1994
2	Cooper	1959 & 1960
2	Brabham	1966 & 1967
1	Vanwall	1958
1	BRM	1962
1	Matra	1969
1	Tyrrell	1971

CONSTRUCTORS' WORLD CHAMPIONSHIP WINNERS 1958-94

Year	Team	Year	Team	Year	Team
1958	Vanwall	1971	Tyrrell	1984	McLaren
1959	Cooper	1972	Lotus	1985	McLaren
1960	Cooper	1973	Lotus	1986	Williams
1961	Ferrari	1974	McLaren	1987	Williams
1962	BRM	1975	Ferrari	1988	McLaren
1963	Lotus	1976	Ferrari	1989	McLaren
1964	Ferrari	1977	Ferrari	1990	McLaren
1965	Lotus	1978	Lotus	1991	McLaren
1966	Brabham	1979	Ferrari	1992	Williams
1967	Brabham	1980	Williams	1993	Williams
1968	Lotus	1981	Williams	1994	Williams
1969	Matra	1982	Ferrari		
1970	Lotus	1983	Ferrari		

GRAND PRIX WINS PER CAR TYPE

Wins	Car Type	Wins	Car Type
104	Ferrari & McLaren	10	Alfa Romeo
79	Lotus	9	Maserati, Matra, Mercedes & Vanwall
78	Williams	8	Ligier
35	Brabham	3	March & Wolf
23	Tyrrell	2	Honda
17	BRM	1	Eagle, Hesketh, Penske, Porche & Shadow
16	Cooper		
15	Renault & Benetton		

GRAND PRIX POLE POSITIONS PER CAR TYPE

Poles	Car Type	Poles	Car Type
113	Ferrari	9	Benetton & Ligier
107	Lotus	8	Mercedes
79	McLaren	7	Vanwall
73	Williams	5	March
39	Brabham	4	Matra
31	Renault	3	Shadow
14	Tyrrell	2	Lancia
12	Alfa Romeo	1	Arrows, Honda, Jordan, Lola, Porsche & Wolf
11	BRM & Cooper		
10	Maserati		

GRAND PRIXS COMPLETED PER CAR TYPE

GP	Car Type	GP	Car Type	GP	Car Type
537	Ferrari	117	Surtees	34	Theodore
490	Lotus	112	Alfa Romeo	33	Porsche
410	McLaren	104	Fittipaldi &	32	Sauber
394	Brabham		Shadow	30	Penske
352	Tyrrell	99	ATS	28	Vanwall
329	Williams	98	Ensign	25	Eagle
293	Ligier	78	Dallara	20	Rial
255	Arrows	69	Maserati	19	Lola Haas
230	March	64	Jordan	17	Onyx
201	Benetton	61	Matra	15	Parnelli
197	BRM	54	Zakspeed	12	Mercedes
155	Minardi	48	AGS,	11	Simtek
139	Lola		Larrousse &	10	Merzario
132	Osella		Wolf	5	Pacific
129	Cooper	40	Gordini	4	Lancia
123	Renault	35	Honda		

GRAND PRIX FASTEST LAPS PER CAR TYPE

Laps	Car Type	Laps	Car Type
119	Ferrari	12	Matra
83	Williams	11	Ligier
71	Lotus	9	Mercedes
69	McLaren	7	March
40	Brabham	6	Vanwall
24	Benetton	4	Surtees
20	Tyrrell	2	Eagle, Honda, Shadow & Wolf
18	Renault	1	Ensign, Gordini, Hesketh, Jordan, Lancia & Parnelli
15	BRM & Maserati		
14	Alfa Romeo		
13	Cooper		

GRAND PRIXS WON BY COUNTRY

Country	Wins	Drivers
Great Britain	156	14
Brazil	79	4
France	77	10
Austria	40	3
Italy	39	13
Argentina	38	3
USA	33	15
Australia	26	2
Germany	13	3
Sweden	12	3
New Zealand	12	2
Belgium	11	2
South Africa	10	1
Switzerland	7	2
Canada	6	1
Finland	5	1
Mexico	2	1

GRAND PRIXS WITH DRIVER FATALITIES

Year	Grand Prix	Venue	Driver	Car	During
1954	Germany	Nurburgring	O. Marimon	Maserati	Practice
1955	Indianapolis	Indianapolis	B. Vukovich		Race
1958	France	Reims	L. Musso	Ferrari	Race
1958	Germany	Nurburgring	P. Collins	Ferrari	Race
1958	Morocco	Casablanca	S. Lewis-Evans	Vanwall	Race
1959	Indianapolis	Indianapolis	J. Unser		Race
			B. Cortner		Race
1960	Belgium	Spa-Fran'	C. Bristow		Race
			A. Stacey		Race
1961	Italy	Monza	Von Trips	Ferrari	Race
1964	Germany	Nurburgring	C. de Beaufor		Practice
1966	Germany	Nurburgring	J. Taylor	Brabham	Race
1967	Monaco	Monaco	L. Bandini	Ferrari	Inj/Race†
1968	France	Rouen	J. Schlesser	Honda	Race
1969	Germany	Nurburgring	G. Mitter		Pactice
1970	Holland	Zandvoort	P. Courage	De Tomaso	Race
1970	Italy	Monza	J. Rindt	Lotus	Practice
1973	Holland	Zandvoort	R. Williamson	March	Race
1973	USA	Watkins Glen	F. Cevert	Tyrrell	Practice
1974	USA	Watkins Glen	H. Koinigg	Surtees	Race
1975	Austria	Osterreichring	M. Donohue	M-Penske	Practice
1977	South Africa	Kyalami	T. Pryce	Shadow	Race
1978	Italy	Monza	R. Peterson	Lotus	Inj/Race*
1982	Belgium	Zolder	G. Villeneuve	Ferrari	Practice
1982	Canada	Montreal	R. Paletti	Osella Ford	Race
1994	San Marino	Imola	R. Ratzenberger	Simtek	Practice
			A. Senna	Williams	Race

† Died three days after race from burns.
* Died the next day from injuries received during start of race.

A-Z
Formula 1 Drivers 94-95

Introduction

These pages contain an A-Z of drivers who have featured in a 1994 Grand Prix or who may feature in a 1995 Grand Prix. While every attempt has been made to ensure that this list is as accurate as possible, new drivers may have come to light after this book went to press. Each entry lists a brief resume of each driver's F1 career to date and then provides a summary of GP details. This is followed by a list of each of the Grand Prix races he has competed in. Numbers in brackets after named Grand Prix signify the number of points scored in the race in question.

Team and Driver Number Allocation 1995

Listed below are the numbers allocated to the teams for the 1995 season and the drivers allocated to the numbers by their team at the time of going to press. Although the team numbers will remain consistent, the numbers allocated to drivers may change, especially when teams are using more than two drivers during the season.

Number	Driver	Country	Team
1	Michael Schumacher	Germany	Benetton
2	Johnny Herbert	Great Britain	Benetton
3	Ukyo Katayama	Japan	Tyrrell
4	Mika Salo	Finland	Tyrrell
5	Damon Hill	Great Britain	Williams
6	David Coulthard	Great Britain	Williams
7	Nigel Mansell/Mark Blundell†	Great Britain	McLaren
8	Mika Hakkinen	Finland	McLaren
9	Gianni Morbidelli	Italy	Arrows
10	Taki Inoue	Japan	Arrows
11	Hideki Noda/	Japan	Simtek
	Domenico Schiattarella	Italy	
12	Jos Verstappen	Holland	Simtek
14	Rubens Barrichello	Brazil	Jordan
15	Eddie Irvine	Great Britain	Jordan
16	Bertrand Gachot	France	Pacific
17	Andrea Montermini/JJ Lehto	Italy/Finland	Pacific
18	Christophe Bouchut	France	Larrousse
19	Eric Helary	France	Larrousse
21	Pedro Paulo Diniz	Brazil	Forti
22	Roberto Moreno†	Brazil	Forti
23	Pierluigi Martini	Italy	Minardi
24	Luca Badoer	Italy	Minardi
25	Martin Brundle/Aguri Suzuki	Great Britain/Japan	Ligier
26	Olivier Panis	France	Ligier
27	Jean Alesi	France	Ferrari
28	Gerhard Berger	Austria	Ferrari
29	Karl Wendlinger	Austria	Sauber
30	Heinz-Harald Frentzen	Germany	Sauber

† Initially for first two Grands Prix only.

ADAMS, Philippe   **Belgium**

Philippe Adams made his F1 debut for troubled Team Lotus last season at
Spa as the Norfolk based team struggled to find drivers with adequate
sponsorship. He qualified in last position on the grid and crashed out of the
race on the 15th lap. His only other race last season saw him finish four laps
down in Portugal. DOB: 19/11/69.

Grand Prix Record

Contested: 2   (1994)
Victories: 0
Fastest laps: 0
Poles: 0

Year	Team	No.	Grand Prix
1994	Lotus Mugen Honda	2	Bel, Por

ALBORETO, Michele   **Italy**

After starting his F1 career with Tyrrell, Michele Alboreto had his most
successful period with Ferrari during the turbo period. After two wins with
the English team in the United States, he had further success in Belgium,
Canada and Germany with his home team as well as a string of podium
finishes. After leaving Ferrari in 1989 he returned to Tyrrell for five races
before spells at Lola and Arrows over the next four years. Last season he
raced for another Italian team in Minardi scoring one World Championship
point for his sixth place in Monaco. DOB: 23/12/56.

Grand Prix Record

Contested: 194   (1981-1994)
Victories: 5   1982 (Veg), 1983 (USAE), 1984 (Bel), 1985 (Can, Ger)
Fastest laps: 4   1982 (Veg), 1985 (San, Mon), 1988 (Ita)
Poles: 2   1984 (Bel), 1985 (Bra)

Year	Team	No.	Grand Prix
1981	Tyrrell Ford	10	San, Bel, Mon, Fra, GB, Aut, Hol, Ita, Can, Veg
1982	Tyrrell Ford	16	SA, Bra (3), USAW (3), San (4), Bel, Mon, USAE, Can, Hol, GB, Fra (1), Ger (3), Aut, Swi, Ita (2), Veg (9)
1983	Tyrrell Ford	15	Bra, USAW, Fra, San, Mon, Bel, USAE (9), Can, GB, Ger, Aut, Hol (1), Ita, Eur, SA

1984	Ferrari Turbo	16	Bra, SA, Bel (9), San, Fra, Mon (1), Can, USAE, Dal, GB (2), Ger, Aut (4), Hol, Ita (6), Eur(6), Por (3)
1985	Ferrari Turbo	16	Bra (6), Por (6), San, Mon (6), Can (9), USAE (4), Fra, GB (6), Ger (9), Aut (4), Hol (3), Ita, Bel, Eur, SA, Aus
1986	Ferrari Turbo	16	Bra, Esp, San, Mon, Bel (3), Can, USAE (3), Fra, GB, Ger, Hun, Aut (6), Ita, Por (2), Mex, Aus
1987	Ferrari Turbo	16	Bra, San (4), Bel, Mon (4), USAE, Fra, GB, Ger, Hun, Aut, Ita, Por, Esp, Mex, Jap (3), Aus (6)
1988	Ferrari Turbo	16	Bra (2), San, Mon (4), Mex (3), Can, USAE, Fra (4), GB, Ger (3), Hun, Bel, Ita (6), Por (2), Esp, Jap, Aus
1989	Tyrrell Ford	5	Bra, Mon (2), Mex (4), USA, Can
	Lola Lamborghini	5	Ger, Hun, Bel, Ita, Por
1990	Arrows Ford	13	USA, Bra, Can, Mex, Fra, GB, Ger, Hun, Bel, Ita, Por, Esp, Jap
1991	Footwork Porsche	4	USA, Mon, Can, Mex
	Footwork Ford	5	Fra, GB, Por, Esp, Aus
1992	Footwork Mugen	16	SA, Mex, Bra (1), Esp (2), San (2), Mon, Can, Fra, GB, Ger, Hun, Bel, Ita, Por (1), Jap, Aus
1993	Lola Ferrari	9	SA, Bra, Eur, Mon, Ger, Hun, Bel, Ita, Por
1994	Minardi Ford	16	Bra, Pac, San, Mon (1), Esp, Can, Fra, GB, Ger, Hun, Bel, Ita, Por, Eur, Jap, Aus

ALESI, Jean   France

This popular French-Sicilian is widely acknowledged as the best driver never to have won a Grand Prix. His highest placing in two seasons with Tyrrell was second in both the United States and Monaco, and in four full seasons with Ferrari he has only equalled that once – in front of the team's own fans at Monza. He has scored consistently since his debut back in 1989, and his fifth place in the Drivers' World Championship with 24 points was his highest placing. He took his only pole position to date at Monza last season, and if his car improves he has the talent to excel. DOB: 11/6/64.

Grand Prix Record
Contested: 85   (1989-1994)
Victories: 0

Fastest laps:	1	1991 (USA)	
Poles:	1	1994 (Ita)	

Year	Team	No.	Grand Prix
1989	Tyrrell Ford	8	Fra (3), GB, Ger, Hun, Ita (2), Esp (3), Jap, Aus
1990	Tyrrell Ford	15	USA (6), Bra, San (1), Mon (6), Can, Mex, Fra, GB, Ger, Hun, Bel, Ita, Por, Esp, Aus
1991	Ferrari	16	USA, Bra (1), San, Mon (4), Can, Mex, Fra (3), GB, Ger (4), Hun (2), Bel, Ita, Por (4), Esp (3), Jap, Aus
1992	Ferrari	16	SA, Mex, Bra (3), Esp (4), San, Mon, Can (4), Fra, GB, Ger (2), Hun, Bel, Ita, Por, Jap (2), Aus (3)
1993	Ferrari	16	SA, Bra, Eur, San, Esp, Mon (4), Can, Fra, GB, Ger, Hun, Bel, Ita (6), Por (3), Jap, Aus (3)
1994	Ferrari	14	Bra (4), Mon (2), Esp (3), Can (4), Fra, GB (6), Ger, Hun, Bel, Ita, Por, Eur, Jap (4), Aus

ALLIOT, Phillippe   France

1994 was a year of only two races for the experienced Frenchman and he
failed to complete either. He deputised for the suspended Mika Hakkinen in
the McLaren in Hungary and occupied the spare seat in the Larrousse in
Belgium. His best finish in a Grand Prix was obtained in 1993 with the
French team when he came fifth in San Marino. He made his debut back in
1984 for the RAM team, and had spells with Ligier and Lola before joining
Larrousse. DOB: 27/7/54.

Grand Prix Record
Contested: 109   (1984-1994)
Victories: 0
Fastest laps: 0
Poles: 0

Year	Team	No.	Grand Prix
1984	RAM Hart Turbo	13	Bra, SA, San, Fra, Can, USAE, GB, Ger, Aut, Hol, Ita, Eur, Por
1985	RAM Hart Turbo	13	Bra, Por, San, Can, USAE, Fra, GB, Ger, Aut, Hol, Ita, Bel, Eur
1986	Ligier Renault Turbo	7	Ger, Hun, Aut, Ita, Por, Mex (1), Aus

1987	Lola Ford	15	San, Bel, Mon, USAE, Fra, GB, Ger (1), Hun, Aut, Ita, Por, Esp (1), Mex (1), Jap, Aus
1988	Lola Ford	16	Bra, San, Mon, Mex, Can, USAE, Fra, GB, Ger, Hun, Bel, Ita, Por, Esp, Jap, Aus
1989	Lola Lamborghini	15	Bra, San, Mon, Mex, USA, Can, Fra, GB, Ger, Bel, Ita, Por, Esp (1), Jap, Aus
1990	Ligier Ford	14	Bra, San, Mon, Can, Mex, Fra, GB, Ger, Hun, Ita, Por, Esp, Jap, Aus
1993	Larrousse Lamborghini	14	SA, Bra, Eur, San (2), Esp, Mon, Can, Fra, GB, Ger, Hun, Bel, Ita, Por
1994	McLaren Peugeot	1	Hun
	Larrousse Ford	1	Bel

BARRICHELLO, Rubens   Brazil

This young Brazilian driver exceeded all expectations last season, only his second in the sport. His sixth place in the Drivers' World Championship with 19 points consisted of half a dozen finishes in the top six including a third at the Pacific Grand Prix at Aida. He finished fourth in Brazil, Britain, Italy, Portugal and Australia, and showed his great tactical awareness at a rain soaked Spa by changing to slicks for the final five minutes of qualifying as the track was still extremely wet. He remains with Jordan for 1995 and could cause many more surprises in his third year. DOB: 23/5/72.

Grand Prix Record

Contested: 31   (1993-94)
Victories: 0
Fastest laps: 0
Poles: 1   1994 (Bel)

Year	Team	No.	Grand Prix
1993	Jordan Hart	16	SA, Bra, Eur, San, Esp, Mon, Can, Fra, GB, Ger, Hun, Bel, Ita, Por, Jap (2), Aus
1994	Jordan Hart	15	Bra (3), Pac (4), Mon, Esp, Can, Fra, GB (3), Ger, Hun, Bel, Ita (3), Por (3), Eur, Jap, Aus (4)

BELMONDO, Jean-Paul   France

Jean-Paul Belmondo's first season in F1 was one of immense frustration. The Frenchman joined the Thetford based Pacific team as they set out in the sport themselves, and despite promising a lot, they delivered very little. Belmondo qualified for only two races in the 1994 season, in Monaco and Spain, and on both occasions this was only due to other teams pulling out of qualifying. He lasted 63 laps in the heat at Monaco before retiring with fatigue, and spun out on lap three in Barcelona. DOB: 23/4/63.

Grand Prix Record

Contested:	7	(1992-94)
Victories:	0	
Fastest laps:	0	
Poles:	0	

Year	Team	No.	Grand Prix
1992	March Ilmor	5	Esp, San, Can, Ger, Hun
1994	Pacific Ilmor	2	Mon, Esp

BERETTA, Olivier   Italy

This Italian's first season in F1 lasted only ten races with the French based Larrousse team as they ran out of money and signed drivers on a race to race basis from Belgium onwards. With the inadequate resources at his disposal, Beretta performed competitively when the engine would let him go the distance. He finished four of his ten starts, with a seventh in his penultimate race at Hockenheim his best placing. DOB: 23/11/69.

Grand Prix Record

Contested:	10	(1994)
Victories:	0	
Fastest laps:	0	
Poles:	0	

Year	Team	No.	Grand Prix
1994	Larrousse Ford	10	Bra, Pac, San, Mon, Esp, Can, Fra, GB, Ger, Hun

BERGER, Gerhard   Austria

The experienced Austrian will start his third season with Ferrari since his return to the Italian team from McLaren in 1993. The reliability of his car was the main reason why he was unable to challenge Schumacher and Hill for the Drivers' Championship last season, and while the Ferrari engine delivered the required speed on the power circuits such as Hockenheim, it was shown up on the more technical tracks. Berger secured his first Grand Prix win with Benetton in 1986, and took four more in his first spell with Ferrari. He moved to McLaren in 1990 and picked up three wins in as many years whilst playing second fiddle to Ayrton Senna. Last season's win in Germany was his first since his return to the Italian team, and his ninth in total. DOB: 27/8/59.

Grand Prix Record

Contested:	163	(1984-1994)	
Victories:	9	1986 (Mex), 1987 (Jap, Aus), 1988 (Ita), 1989 (Por), 1991 (Jap), 1992 (Can, Aus), 1994 (Ger)	
Fastest laps:	16	1986 (Ger, Aut), 1987 (Por, Esp, Aus), 1988 (Bra, Bel, Por), 1989 (Por), 1990 (Bra, USA, Can), 1991 (San, Aus), 1992 (Mex, Can)	
Poles:	9	1987 (Por, Jap, Aus), 1988 (GB), 1990 (USA, Mex), 1991 (Esp, Jap), 1994 (Por)	

Year	Team	No.	Grand Prix
1984	ATS BMW Turbo	4	Aut, Ita, Eur, Por
1985	Arrows BMW Turbo	16	Bra, Por, San, Mon, Can, USAE, Fra, GB, Ger, Aut, Hol, Ita, Bel, Eur, SA (2), Aus (1)
1986	Benetton BMW Turbo	16	Bra (1), Esp (1), San (4), Mon, Bel, Can, USAE, Fra, GB, Ger, Hun, Aut, Ita (2), Por, Mex (9), Aus
1987	Ferrari Turbo	16	Bra (3), San, Bel, Mon (3), USAE (3), Fra, GB, Ger, Hun, Aut, Ita (3), Por (6), Esp, Mex, Jap (9), Aus (9)
1988	Ferrari Turbo	16	Bra (6), San (2), Mon (6), Mex (4), Can, USAE, Fra (3), GB, Ger (4), Hun (3), Bel, Ita (9), Por, Esp (1), Jap (3), Aus
1989	Ferrari	15	Bra, San, Mex, USA, Can, Fra, GB, Ger, Hun, Bel, Ita (6), Por (9), Esp (6), Jap, Aus
1990	McLaren Honda	16	USA, Bra (6), San (6), Mon (4), Can (3), Mex (4), Fra (2), GB, Ger (4), Hun, Bel (4), Ita (4), Por (3), Esp, Jap, Aus (3)
1991	McLaren Honda	16	USA, Bra (4), San (6), Mon, Can, Mex, Fra, GB (6), Ger (3), Hun (3), Bel (6), Ita (3), Por, Esp, Jap (9), Aus (4)
1992	McLaren Honda	16	SA (2), Mex (3), Bra, Esp (3), San, Mon, Can (10), Fra, GB (2), Ger, Hun (4), Bel, Ita (3), Por (6), Jap (6), Aus (10)
1993	Ferrari	16	SA (1), Bra, Eur, San, Esp (1), Mon, Can (3), Fra, GB, Ger (1), Hun (4), Bel, Ita, Por, Jap, Aus (2)

| 1994 | Ferrari | 16 | Bra, Pac (6), San, Mon (4), Esp, Can (3), Fra (4), GB, Ger (10), Hun, Bel, Ita (6), Por, Eur (2), Jap, Aus (6) |

BERNARD, Eric   France

After three years with Lola, Eric Bernard returned to F1 last season with Ligier after a two year absence from the sport and achieved his highest ever finish of third in the German Grand Prix at Hockenheim. He took his car home for a place on the podium aided largely by eleven cars crashing out of the race at the very first corner. Narrowly missing out on a further point in Italy, the rest of his finishes were between three and six places further down, and prior to the European Grand Prix at Jerez he was swapped by the French team and joined Team Lotus as Johnny Herbert made the opposite journey. He raced only once for the Thetford based team. DOB: 26/8/64.

Grand Prix Record

Contested: 45   (1989-1994)
Victories: 0
Fastest laps: 0
Poles: 0

Year	Team	No.	Grand Prix
1989	Lola Lamborghini	2	Fra, GB
1990	Lola Lamborghini	16	USA, Bra, San, Mon (1), Can, Mex, Fra, GB (3), Ger, Hun (1), Bel, Ita, Por, Esp, Jap, Aus
1991	Lola Ford	13	USA, Bra, San, Mon, Can, Mex (1), Fra, GB, Ger, Hun, Bel, Ita, Esp
1994	Ligier Renault	13	Bra, Pac, San, Mon, Esp, Can, Fra, GB, Ger (4), Hun, Bel, Ita, Por
	Lotus Mugen Honda	1	Eur

BLUNDELL, Mark   Great Britain

Mark Blundell joined Tyrrell from Ligier at the start of 1994 after he had claimed two podium finishes with the French team the previous season. A further third place was obtained in Barcelona, with consecutive fifth placings at Hungary and Belgium making up his total of eight World Championship points and 12th place. After his debut season with Brabham in 1991, he returned with fellow Englishman Martin Brundle to Ligier after a year's break from the sport, and came in for criticism from the French press when the Magny-Cours based team failed to sign a French driver. DOB: 8/4/66.

Grand Prix Record

Contested: 46 (1991-1994)
Victories: 0
Fastest laps: 0
Poles: 0

Year	Team	No.	Grand Prix
1991	Brabham Yamaha	14	USA, Bra, San, Mon, Mex, Fra, GB, Ger, Hun, Bel (1), Ita, Por, Esp, Aus
1993	Ligier Renault	16	SA (4), Bra (2), Eur, San, Esp, Mon, Can, Fra, GB, Ger (4), Hun, Bel, Ita, Por, Jap, Aus
1994	Tyrrell Yamaha	16	Bra, Pac, San, Mon, Esp (4), Can, Fra, GB, Ger, Hun (2), Bel (2), Ita, Por, Eur, Jap, Aus

BRABHAM, David   Australia

It's often difficult to follow in your father's footsteps, and David Brabham knows that he still has a lot to do if he is to emulate his father Jack. 1994 was not a good year for the young Australian, when his car gave him trouble all season with retirements through engine, brakes, gearbox, clutch and steering. His highest placing in the season was tenth in Spain and was one of only six finishes all season. DOB: 5/9/65.

Grand Prix Record

Contested: 22 (1990-1994)
Victories: 0
Fastest laps: 0
Poles: 0

Year	Team	No.	Grand Prix
1990	Brabham Judd	6	Bra, Mex, Bel, Por, Jap, Aus
1994	Simtek Ford	16	Bra, Pac, San, Mon, Esp, Can, Fra, GB, Ger, Hun, Bel, Ita, Por, Eur, Jap, Aus

BRUNDLE, Martin   Great Britain

Martin Brundle held out for a seat at McLaren in 1994 and his patience was rewarded. He took a gamble and it paid off with a drive for the season, although the Peugeot engine was not perhaps what he was expecting. More than half his retirements were due to the new engine, and in Britain it failed before the race had even started. Brundle came second to Schumacher in Monaco and picked up the other 10 of his 16 points with third, fourth, fifth and sixth at Australia, Hungary, Italy and Portugal respectively. Last season's result in Monaco matched his best finish in Italy with Benetton in 1992. He made his debut for Tyrrell before moving to Zakspeed and Brabham. After a year with Benetton he joined Ligier before moving to McLaren. DOB: 1/6/59.

Grand Prix Record

Contested: 131   (1984-1994)
Victories: 0
Fastest laps: 0
Poles: 0

Year	Team	No.	Grand Prix
1984	Tyrrell Ford	7	Bra, SA, Bel, San, Fra, Can, USAE
1985	Tyrrell Ford	7	Bra, Por, San, Mon, Can, USAE, Ger
	Tyrrell Renault Turbo	8	Fra, GB, Hol, Ita, Bel, Eur, SA, Aus
1986	Tyrrell Renault Turbo	16	Bra (2), Esp, San, Mon, Bel, Can, USAE, Fra, GB (2), Ger, Hun (1), Aut, Ita, Por, Mex, Aus (3)
1987	Zakspeed Turbo	16	Bra, San (2), Bel, Mon, USAE, Fra, GB, Ger, Hun, Aut, Ita, Por, Esp, Mex, Jap, Aus
1988	Williams Judd	1	Bel
1989	Brabham Judd	14	Bra, San, Mon (1), Mex, USA, GB, Ger, Hun, Bel, Ita (1), Por, Esp, Jap (2), Aus
1991	Brabham Yamaha	14	USA, Bra, San, Can, Mex, Fra, GB, Ger, Hun, Bel, Ita, Por, Esp, Jap (2)
1992	Benetton Ford	16	SA, Mex, Bra, Esp, San (3), Mon (2), Can, Fra (4), GB (4), Ger (3), Hun (2), Bel (3), Ita (6), Por (3), Jap (4), Aus (4)
1993	Ligier Renault	16	SA, Bra, Eur, San (4), Esp, Mon (1), Can (2), Fra (2), GB, Ger, Hun (2), Bel, Ita, Por (1), Jap, Aus (1)
1994	McLaren Peugeot	16	Bra, Pac, San, Mon (6), Esp, Can, Fra, GB, Ger, Hun (3), Bel, Ita (2), Por (1), Eur, Jap, Aus (4)

COMAS, Erik   France

Erik Comas made his F1 debut for Ligier in 1991, and completed his second season with Larrousse in 1994. He picked up two sixth place finishes last year at Aida and Hockenheim to add to sixth in Italy with Larrousse the year before. He came sixth twice whilst with Ligier for two years and his best finish to date was fifth at his home Grand Prix back in 1992. DOB: 28/9/63.

Grand Prix Record

Contested: 59   (1991-1994)
Victories: 0
Fastest laps: 0
Poles: 0

Year	Team	No.	Grand Prix
1991	Ligier Lamborghini	13	Bra, San, Mon, Can, Fra, Ger, Hun, Bel, Ita, Por, Esp, Jap, Aus
1992	Ligier Renault	15	SA, Mex, Bra, Esp, San, Mon, Can (1), Fra (2), GB, Ger (1), Hun, Ita, Por, Jap, Aus
1993	Larrousse Lamborghini	16	SA, Bra, Eur, San, Esp, Mon, Can, Fra, GB, Ger, Hun, Bel, Ita (1), Por, Jap, Aus
1994	Larrousse Ford	15	Bra, Pac (1), San, Mon, Esp, Can, Fra, GB, Ger (1), Hun, Bel, Ita, Por, Eur, Jap

COULTHARD, David   Great Britain

From test driver to likely Championship contender in just a few months? The young Scotsman showed extreme maturity as he stepped in to fill the gap in the Williams team last year left by the death of Ayrton Senna. He picked up his first points in Canada with fifth place and returned to do the same at Silverstone having been replaced for the French Grand Prix by Nigel Mansell. He set the fastest lap at Hockenheim before retiring, and did the same at Estoril as he came home behind team-mate Damon Hill. Mansell returned for the final three races of the season, but Coulthard has been reward for the potential he showed by being given the second Williams seat for 1995 ahead of Mansell. A young man who can only get better but still with it all to do!
DOB: 27/3/71.

Grand Prix Record

Contested: 8   (1994)
Victories: 0
Fastest laps: 2   1994 (Ger, Por)
Poles: 0

Year	Team	No.	Grand Prix
1994	Williams Renault	8	Esp, Can (2), GB (2), Ger, Hun, Bel (3), Ita (1), Por (6)

DALMAS, Yannick   France

The Frenchman had sponsorship and the French team had none. Dalmas drove two races for Larrousse in 1994 and did little to be noticed in either Italy or Portugal. It was his first race in F1 for four seasons since he drove five times for AGS in 1990. His sole points finish came in only his third race of his career when he finished fifth in Australia whilst with Lola for whom he drove for three seasons. DOB: 28/7/61.

Grand Prix Record

Contested: 24   (1987-1994)
Victories: 0
Fastest laps: 0
Poles: 0

Year	Team	No.	Grand Prix
1987	Lola Ford	3	Mex, Jap, Aus (2)
1988	Lola Ford	13	Bra, San, Mon, Mex, USAE, Fra, GB, Ger, Hun, Bel, Ita, Por, Esp
1989	Lola Lamborghini	1	San
1990	AGS Ford	5	Bra, Fra, Ita, Por, Esp
1994	Larrousse Ford	2	Ita, Por

de CESARIS, Andrea   Italy

Last season's Canadian Grand Prix in Montreal saw this experienced Italian race in his 200th Grand Prix with his tenth team. He reached his 199th with two races filling in for the suspended Eddie Irvine in the Jordan and picked up three points for fourth in Monaco. He then replaced the injured Karl Wendlinger for Sauber and took a point in France with the only finish of his nine races for the Swiss team. He made his debut back in 1980 for Alfa Romeo and has also driven for McLaren, Ligier, Brabham and Tyrrell to name but a few. He took pole in the United States in his second stint at Alfa in 1982, and picked up his best finishes with the same team the following year with second in Germany and South Africa. DOB: 31/5/59.

Grand Prix Record

Contested: 208 (1980-1994)
Victories: 0
Fastest laps: 1   1983 (Bel)
Poles: 1   1982 (USAW)

Year	Team	No.	Grand Prix
1980	Alfa Romeo	2	Can, USAE
1981	McLaren Ford	14	USAW, Bra, Arg, San (1), Bel, Mon, Esp, Fra, GB, Ger, Aut, Ita, Can, Veg

1982	Alfa Romeo	16	SA, Bra, USAW, San, Bel, Mon (4), USAE, Can (1), Hol, GB, Fra, Ger, Aut, Swi, Ita, Veg
1983	Alfa Romeo Turbo	14	USAW, Fra, San, Mon, Bel, USAE, Can, GB, Ger (6), Aut, Hol, Ita, Eur (3), SA (6)
1984	Ligier Renault Turbo	16	Bra, SA (2), Bel, San (1), Fra, Mon, Can, USAE, Dal, GB, Ger, Aut, Hol, Ita, Eur, Por
1985	Ligier Renault Turbo	11	Bra, Por, San, Mon (3), Can, USAE, Fra, GB, Ger, Aut, Hol
1986	Minardi MM Turbo	15	Bra, Esp, San, Bel, Can, USAE, Fra, GB, Ger, Hun, Aut, Ita, Por, Mex, Aus
1987	Brabham BMW Turbo	16	Bra, San, Bel (4), Mon, USAE, Fra, GB, Ger, Hun, Aut, Ita, Por, Esp, Mex, Jap, Aus
1988	Rial Ford	16	Bra, San, Mon, Mex, Can, USAE (3), Fra, GB, Ger, Hun, Bel, Ita, Por, Esp, Jap, Aus
1989	Dallara Ford	15	Bra, Ger, Mon, Mex, USA, Can (4), GB, Ger, Hun, Bel, Ita, Por, Esp, Jap, Aus
1990	Dallara Ford	15	USA, Bra, San, Mon, Can, Mex, Fra, GB, Hun, Bel, Ita, Por, Esp, Jap, Aus
1991	Jordan Ford	15	Bra, San, Mon, Can (3), Mex (3), Fra (1), GB, Ger (2), Hun, Bel, Ita, Por, Esp, Jap, Aus
1992	Tyrrell Ilmor	16	SA, Mex (2), Bra, Esp, San, Mon, Can (2), Fra, GB, Ger, Hun, Bel, Ita (1), Por, Jap (3), Aus
1993	Tyrrell Yamaha	16	SA, Bra, Eur, San, Esp, Mon, Can, Fra, GB, Ger, Hun, Bel, Ita, Por, Jap, Aus
1994	Jordan Hart	2	San, Mon (3)
	Sauber Mercedes	9	Can, Fra (1), GB, Ger, Hun, Bel, Ita, Por, Eur

DELETRAZ, Jean-Denis   France

If you have sponsorship and a F1 team is short of money, then there is a good chance you might get a race. That's exactly what happen for Jean-Denis Deletraz at the Australian Grand Prix. He drove for the Larrousse team, he qualified 25th and retired with gearbox trouble on lap 56. DOB: 1/10/63.

Grand Prix Record

Contested:	1	(1994)
Victories:	0	
Fastest laps:	0	
Poles:	0	

Year	Team	No.	Grand Prix
1994	Larrousse Ford	1	Aus

DENIZ, Pedro   Brazil

This 24 year-old Brazilian will make his F1 debut at his home Grand Prix at the end of March. He has a reputation for not reaching the end of races through driver error, and will be driving for the Forti team with a Ford Cosworth engine as they too make their F1 debut at Interlagos. DOB:22/5/70.

Grand Prix Record

Contested:	0
Victories:	0
Fastest laps:	0
Poles:	0

FITTIPALDI, Christian   Brazil

The third of the Fittipaldi's to race in F1, Christian follows father Wilson and uncle Emerson into the sport. Last year with Arrows was only his third full season, having raced the previous two years with Minardi. Racing with the Milton Keynes based team and driving a Footwork car, he came fourth in the second race of the season at the Pacific Grand Prix in Aida. He thought he had picked up a point for sixth in Montreal, but he was later disqualified when his car was found to be underweight. His fourth place in Aida was repeated in Germany after he managed to avoid the first corner incident that took eleven cars out of the race. The 1994 results added to a fourth, fifth and sixth with Minardi over the previous two seasons. DOB: 18/1/71.

Grand Prix Record

Contested:	40	(1992-1994)
Victories:	0	
Fastest laps:	0	
Poles:	0	

Year	Team	No.	Grand Prix
1992	Minardi Lamborghini	10	SA, Mex, Bra, Esp, San, Mon, Can, Por, Jap (1), Aus

| 1993 | Minardi Ford | 14 | SA (3), Bra, Eur, San, Esp, Mon (2), Can, Fra, GB, Ger, Hun, Bel, Ita, Por |
| 1994 | Footwork Ford | 16 | Bra, Pac (3), San, Mon, Esp, Can, Fra, GB, Ger (3), Hun, Bel, Ita, Por, Eur, Jap, Aus |

FRENTZEN, Heinz-Harald   Germany

When the Sauber finished a race, Heinz-Harald Frentzen could be found between fourth and seventh. Frentzen finished seven races, retired from eight and did not start in Monaco after Karl Wendlinger's crash. The German's first season in F1 would probably have received greater publicity in his home country had Michael Schumacher not taken the Drivers' Championship, but 13th place with seven points was extremely creditable. His best finish was fourth in France, with fifth at Aida and sixth at consecutive races at Jerez and Suzuka. With fifteen races now behind him, more of the same can be expected for 1995. DOB: 18/5/67.

Grand Prix Record
Contested: 15   (1994)
Victories: 0
Fastest laps: 0
Poles: 0

Year	Team	No.	Grand Prix
1994	Sauber Mercedes	15	Bra, Pac (2), San, Esp, Can, Fra (3), GB, Ger, Hun, Bel, Ita, Por, Eur (1), Jap (1), Aus

GACHOT, Bertrand   France

Only qualifying for five of last year's races tells its own sorry story for the Frenchman. He joined the newly formed Pacific team after a year out of the sport, and to an extent his sabbatical has now extended to two years. Qualification was gained in five of the first six races, but for the last ten Grand Prix Bertrand Gachot watched as a spectator. His best time was spent at Jordan in 1991 when he came fifth in Canada and sixth in Germany and Britain. Sixth place was also achieved with Larrousse in 1992 in Monaco, three years after his debut for Onyx. DOB: 22/12/62.

Grand Prix Record
Contested: 36   (1989–1994)
Victories: 0
Fastest laps: 1   1991 (Hun)
Poles: 0

Year	Team	No.	Grand Prix
1989	Onyx-Ford	5	Fra, GB, Hun, Bel, Ita
1991	Jordan Ford	10	USA, Bra, San, Mon, Can (2), Mex, Fra, GB (1), Ger (1), Hun
1992	Larrousse-Venturi Lamborghini	16	SA, Mex, Bra, Esp, San, Mon (1), Can Fra, GB, Ger, Hun, Bel, Ita, Por, Jap, Aus
1994	Pacific Ilmor	5	Bra, San, Esp, Can, Fra

GOUNON, Jean-Marc   France

Jean-Marc Gounon came into F1 to join the new Simtek team after they had been decimated by two horrific accidents. The Frenchman replaced the injured Andrea Montermini after the Italian had come in following the death of Roland Ratzenberger. Gounon took part in seven races during the middle part of the 1994 season with his best placing being ninth on his debut in France. He retired in three of the other six races he started. DOB: 1/1/63.

Grand Prix Record
Contested: 7   (1994)
Victories: 0
Fastest laps: 0
Poles: 0

Year	Team	No.	Grand Prix
1994	Simtek Ford	7	Fra, GB, Ger, Hun, Bel, Ita, Por

HAKKINEN, Mika   Finland

Mika Hakkinen took his tally of podium finishes to seven with six top three results in 1994. Only two of his seven retirements were down to driver error, although his rash actions at the start of the German Grand Prix led to a one race ban with almost half the field wiped out at the start. He picked up two third placings in the first half of the season at Imola and Silverstone, and after his crash and subsequent ban, he finished the last six races of the season with a run of four consecutive podium finishes with second at Spa, and third at Monza, Estoril and Jerez. He joined McLaren from Lotus where he had seven points finishes in his two years with the Norfolk based team. DOB: 28/9/68.

Grand Prix Record
Contested: 48   (1991-1994)
Victories: 0
Fastest laps: 0
Poles: 0

Year	Team	No.	Grand Prix
1991	Lotus Judd	15	USA, Bra, San (2), Mon, Can, Mex, GB, Ger, Hun, Bel, Ita, Por, Esp, Jap, Aus
1992	Lotus Ford	15	SA, Mex (1), Bra, Esp, Mon, Can, Fra (3), GB (1), Ger, Hun (3), Bel (1), Ita, Por (2), Jap, Aus
1993	McLaren Ford	3	Por, Jap (4), Aus
1994	McLaren Peugeot	15	Bra, Pac, San (4), Mon, Esp, Can, Fra, GB (4), Ger, Bel (6), Ita (4), Por, Eur, Jap, Aus

HERBERT, Johnny   Great Britain

Johnny Herbert made a sensation debut in 1989 when he finished fourth in his first Grand Prix for Benetton in Brazil. He followed that with a fifth place in the United States before a switch to Tyrrell and then Lotus where he remained for four years. He picked up six point scoring finishes in that period including fourth at Brazil, Europe and Britain in 1993. Last year was not a good one for the young Englishman. Team Lotus had acquired the Mugen-Honda engine, but after narrowly missing out on a top six finish on four occasions, he left the troubled Norfolk outfit and joined Ligier. After just one race with the French team he was switched to sister team Benetton in a bid to score points to aid their bid for the Constructors' World Championship, but he failed to finish in the last two races of the season in Japan and Australia. DOB: 27/6/64.

Grand Prix Record

Contested: 63   (1989-1994)
Victories: 0
Fastest laps: 0
Poles: 0

Year	Team	No.	Grand Prix
1989	Benetton Ford	5	Bra (3), San, Mon, Mex, USA (2)
	Tyrrell Ford	1	Bel
1990	Lotus Lamborghini	2	Jap, Aus
1991	Lotus Judd	7	Mex, Fra, GB, Bel, Por, Jap, Aus
1992	Lotus Ford	16	SA (1), Mex, Bra, Esp, San, Mon, Can, Fra (1), GB, Ger, Hun, Bel, Ita, Por, Jap, Aus
1993	Lotus Ford	16	SA, Bra (3), Eur (3), San, Esp, Mon, Can, Fra, GB (3), Ger, Hun, Bel (2), Ita, Por, Jap, Aus

1994	Lotus Mugen Honda	13	Bra, Pac, San, Mon, Esp, Can, Fra, GB, Ger, Hun, Bel, Ita, Por
	Ligier Renault	1	Eur
	Benetton Ford	2	Jap, Aus

HILL, Damon   Great Britain

So near and yet so far for Damon Hill in 1994. Half way through the season, few people would have given him any chance of emulating his father Graham, but the fact that he lost the Drivers' World Championship by just one point was a testament to his driving abilities apart from Michael Schumacher's off the track problems. After just two races with the disappointing Brabham team in 1992, he supported Alain Prost's third World Championship in the second Williams in 1993 and won successive Grand Prix in Hungary, Italy and Portugal to finish third in the drivers' standings. Following the death of Ayrton Senna at Imola, the position of team leader was thrust upon him, and after wins at Barcelona and Silverstone he repeated the feat of three straight wins in Belgium, Italy and Portugal to re-enter the race for the title. His win in Japan, his sixth of the season and his ninth in total, took the Drivers' Championship to the final race of the season in Australia. His collision with Michael Schumacher on the 35th lap at Adelaide ended his chances of the title, but he'll be stronger, and no doubt even more determined, in 1995. DOB: 7/9/60.

Grand Prix Record

Contested:	34	(1992-1994)	
Victories:	9	1993 (Hun, Bel, Ita), 1994 (Esp, GB, Bel, Ita, Por, Jap)	
Fastest laps:	10	1993 (GB, Ita, Por, Aus). 1994 (San, Fra, GB, Bel, Ita, Jap)	
Poles:	4	1993 (Fra, Por), 1994 (Fra, GB)	

Year	Team	No.	Grand Prix
1992	Brabham Judd	2	GB, Hun
1993	Williams Renault	16	SA, Bra (6), Eur (6), San, Esp, Mon (6), Can (4), Fra (6), GB, Ger, Hun (10), Bel (10, Ita (10, Por (4), Jap (3), Aus (4)
1994	Williams Renault	16	Bra (6), Pac, San (1), Mon, Esp (10), Can (6), Fra (6), GB (10), Ger, Hun (6), Bel (10), Ita (10), Por (10), Eur (6), Jap (10), Aus

INOUE, Takachiho · Japan

One race, one retirement. Taki Inoue stepped into a vacant seat at Simtek for the penultimate race of the 1994 season at Suzuka for no other reason than to enable his sponsors to see a Japanese driver in the Japanese GP. DOB: 5/9/63.

Grand Prix Record

Contested:	1	(1994)
Victories:	0	
Fastest laps:	0	
Poles:	0	

Year	Team	No.	Grand Prix
1994	Simtek Ford	1	Jap

IRVINE, Eddie · Great Britain

Eddie Irvine attracts attention. He took a point on his F1 debut in Japan in 1993 but got on the wrong side of Ayrton Senna in the next race with his aggressive driving style. He was involved in a four car collision during the Brazilian Grand Prix at the start of last season, and was blamed for the incident and banned for one race. He took it to appeal and had the suspension increased to three races. After his ban and a number of retirements, Irvine picked up three top six finishes with fourth in Europe, fifth in Japan and sixth in Spain. He has formed a good partnership with team-mate Rubens Barrichello and providing he can stay out of trouble, he should have a good 1995. DOB: 10/11/65.

Grand Prix Record

Contested:	15	(1993-94)
Victories:	0	
Fastest laps:	0	
Poles:	0	

Year	Team	No.	Grand Prix
1993	Jordan Hart	2	Jap (1), Aus
1994	Jordan Hart	13	Bra, Esp (1), Can, Fra, GB, Ger, Hun, Bel, Ita, Por, Eur (3), Jap (2), Aus

KATAYAMA, Ukyo · Japan

The top Japanese driver of the season was good when he finished the races. Seven of his twelve retirements were down to technical problems, and his four finishes ranged from fifth to seventh. Brazil and San Marino provided two points apiece with his other points finish of sixth at Silverstone. He joined Tyrrell from Larrousse in 1993, and the points he scored this season were his first in the World Championship. DOB: 29/5/63.

Grand Prix Record

Contested: 46   (1992-1994)
Victories: 0
Fastest laps: 0
Poles: 0

Year	Team	No.	Grand Prix
1992	Larrousse-Venturi Lamborghini		
		14	SA, Mex, Bra, San, Can, Fra, GB, Ger, Hun, Bel, Ita, Por, Jap, Aus
1993	Tyrrell Yamaha	16	SA, Bra, Eur, San, Esp, Mon, Can, Fra, GB, Ger, Hun, Bel, Ita, Por, Jap, Aus
1994	Tyrrell Yamaha	16	Bra (2), Pac, San (2), Mon, Esp, Can, Fra, GB (1), Ger, Hun, Bel, Ita, Por, Eur, Jap, Aus

LAMY, Pedro   Portugal

The only Portuguese driver in the 1994 World Championship drove only in the first four races. He made his debut for Lotus the season before when he replaced the injured Alessandro Zanardi for the last four races of the 1993 season. He finished 8th, 10th and 11th in Aida, Interlagos and Monaco respectively, and retired in Imola following a first lap accident. DOB: 20/3/72.

Grand Prix Record

Contested: 8   (1993-1994)
Victories: 0
Fastest laps: 0
Poles: 0

Year	Team	No.	Grand Prix
1993	Lotus Ford	4	Ita, Por, Jap, Aus
1994	Lotus Mugen Honda	4	Bra, Pac, San, Mon

LAGORCE, Franck   France

Franck Lagorce drove in the last two Grand Prix of 1994 for the French Ligier team after Johnny Herbert was pinched by sister team Benetton. He qualified in 20th position for both Japan and Australia, spinning at Suzuka and finishing two laps down at Adelaide. DOB: 1/9/68.

Grand Prix Record

Contested: 2   (1994)
Victories: 0
Fastest laps: 0
Poles: 0

Year	Team	No.	Grand Prix
1994	Ligier Renault	2	Jap, Aus

LARINI, Nicola   Italy

Ferrari's test driver in 1994, Nicola Larini drove in place of the injured Jean Alesi in the Pacific and San Marino Grand Prix. He retired in Aida, but at Imola he ended the worst run of failing to score a point, 43 races, when he took second behind Michael Schumacher. Unfortunately, few people will remember his achievement due to other circumstances that weekend. In 1995 he returns as test driver and will be a more than adeqaute deputy for either Jean Alesi or Gerhard Berger. DOB: 19/3/64.

Grand Prix Record

Contested: 44   (1987-1994)
Victories: 0
Fastest laps: 0
Poles: 0

Year	Team	No.	Grand Prix
1987	Coloni	5	Por, Esp, Mex, Jap, Aus
1988	Osella Alpha Romeo Turbo	10	Mon, USAE, Fra, GB, Ger, Bel, Ita, Por, Esp, Jap
1989	Osella Turbo	9	Bra, San, Can, GB, Hun, Ita, Esp, Jap, Aus
1990	Ligier-Ford	16	USA, Bra, San, Mon, Can, Mex, Fra, GB, Ger, Hun, Bel, Ita, Por, Esp, Jap, Aus
1992	Ferrari	2	Jap, Aus
1994	Ferrari	2	Pac, San (6)

LEHTO, JJ (Jyrki Jarvilehto)   Finland

Four seasons, split evenly between Onyx and Dallara, occupied the first four years of JJ Lehto's F1 career with the highlight a third place in San Marino with Dallara in 1991. He picked up a fourth and a fifth at San Marino and South Africa with the new Sauber team in 1993 and drove in the last two races of 1994 for the Swiss outfit. His only point last year came with sixth place in Canada in one of only four races for Benetton. DOB: 31/1/66.

Grand Prix Record

Contested: 60   (1989-1994)
Victories: 0
Fastest laps: 0
Poles: 0

Year	Team	No.	Grand Prix
1989	Onyx Ford	2	Esp, Aus
1990	Onyx Ford	5	San, Mon, Can, Mex, Ger
1991	Dallara Judd	16	USA, Bra, San (4), Mon, Can, Mex, Fra, GB, Ger, Hun, Bel, Ita, Por, Esp, Jap, Aus
1992	Dallara Ferrari	15	SA, Mex, Bra, Esp, San, Mon, Can, Fra, GB, Ger, Bel, Ita, Por, Jap, Aus
1993	Sauber	16	SA (2), Bra, Eur, San (3), Esp, Mon, Can, Fra, GB, Ger, Hun, Bel, Ita, Por, Jap, Aus
1994	Benetton Ford	4	San, Mon, Esp, Can (1)
	Sauber Mercedes	2	Jap, Aus

MANSELL, Nigel   Great Britain

The 1992 World Drivers' Champion returned to F1 for four guest appearances in the Williams during the 1994 season. The situation came about with Nigel Mansell unhappy in his second season in the Indy Car Championship, and Frank Williams desperate search to find a high profile figure to put in his car following the very public death of Ayrton Senna. Mansell returned for the French Grand Prix at Magny-Cours but went off. Returning for the last three races of the year, he retired once again in Jerez, finished fourth in Suzuka and won in Adelaide after Schumacher and Hill had collided. Mansell started his career with Lotus before his initial move to Williams, and after narrowly missing out on the Drivers' Championship in both 1986 and 1987, he switched to Ferrari in 1989. Returning to Williams in 1991, he finished second to Ayrton Senna before taking the title the following season, winning a record nine races in the season. He made the transition to Indy Cars as he passed by the chance to defend his title, and won the PPG World Series in his rookie year. DOB: 8/8/53.

Grand Prix Record

Contested: 185 (1980-1994)

Victories: 31 1985 (Eur, SA), 1986 (Bel, Can, Fra, GB, Por), 1987 (San, Fra, GB, Aut, Esp, Mex), 1989 (Bra, Hun), 1990 (Por), 1991 (Fra, GB, Ger, Ita, Esp), 1992 (SA, Mex, Bra, Esp, San, Fra, GB, Ger, Por), 1994 (Aus)

Fastest laps: 30 1983 (Eur), 1985 (Ita), 1986 (Esp, Fra, GB, Por), 1987 (GB, Ger, Aut), 1988 (GB), 1989 (Mex, GB, Hun), 1990 (Fra, GB, Aus), 1991 (Bra, Can, Mex, Fra, GB, Por), 1992 (SA, Esp, Mon, Fra, GB, Hun, Ita, Jap)

Poles: 32 1984 (Dal), 1985 (SA), 1986 (Can, Aus), 1987 (Bra, Bel, Mon, USAE, Fra, Ger, Hun, Mex), 1990 (Fra, GB, Por), 1991 (GB, Ger), 1992 (SA, Mex, Bra, Esp, San, Mon, Fra, GB, Ger, Bel, Ita, Por, Jap, Aus), 1994 (Aus)

Year	Team	No.	Grand Prix
1980	Lotus Ford	2	Aut, Hol
1981	Lotus Ford	13	USAW, Bra, Arg, Bel (4), Mon, Esp (1), Fra, Ger, Aut, Hol, Ita, Can, Veg (3)
1982	Lotus Ford	13	SA, Bra (4), USAW, Bel, Mon (3), USAE, Can, GB, Ger, Aut, Swi, Ita, Veg
1983	Lotus Ford	8	Bra, USAW, Fra, San, Mon, Bel, USAE (1), Can
	Lotus Renault Turbo	7	GB (3), Ger, Aut (2), Hol, Ita, Eur (4), SA
1984	Lotus Renault Turbo	16	Bra, SA, Bel, San, Fra (4), Mon, Can (1), USAE, Dal (1), GB (3), Ger, Aut, Hol (4), Ita, Eur, Por
1985	Williams Honda Turbo	15	Bra, Por (2), San (2), Mon, Can (1), USAE, GB, Ger (1), Aut, Hol (1), Ita, Bel (6), Eur (9), SA (9), Aus
1986	Williams Honda Turbo	16	Bra, Esp (6), San, Mon (3), Bel (9), Can (9), USAE (2), Fra (9), GB (9), Ger (4), Hun (4), Aut, Ita (6), Por (9), Mex (2), Aus
1987	Williams Honda Turbo	14	Bra (1), San (9), Bel, Mon, USAE (2), Fra (9), GB (9), Ger, Hun, Aut (9), Ita (4), Por, Esp (9), Mex (9)
1988	Williams Judd	14	Bra, San, Mon, Mex, Can, USAE, Fra, GB (6), Ger, Hun, Por, Esp (6), Jap, Aus
1989	Ferrari	15	Bra (9), San, Mon, Mex, USA, Can, Fra (6), GB (6), Ger (4), Hun (9), Bel

Year	Team	No.	Grand Prix
			(4), Ita, Por, Jap, Aus
1990	Ferrari	16	USA, Bra (3), San, Mon, Can (4), Mex (6), Fra, GB, Ger, Hun, Bel, Ita (3), Por (9), Esp (6), Jap, Aus (6)
1991	Williams Renault	16	USA, Bra, San, Mon (6), Can (1), Mex (6), Fra (9), GB (9), Ger (9), Hun (6), Bel, Ita (9), Por, Esp (9), Jap, Aus (6)
1992	Williams Renault	16	SA (10), Mex (10), Bra (10), Esp (10), San (10), Mon (6), Can, Fra (10), GB (10), Ger (10), Hun (6), Bel (6), Ita, Por (10), Jap, Aus
1994	Williams Renault	4	Fra, Eur, Jap (3), Aus (10)

MARTINI, Pierluigi   Italy

With the exception of a year with Dallara in 1992, Pierluigi Martini has driven exclusively for Minardi. 1994 saw him take four World Championship points from two fifth places in Spain and France with finishes in more than half of the sixteen races. He made his debut in 1985 and his best performance came in qualifying in the United States in 1990 where he shared the front row of the grid with the McLaren of Gerhard Berger. His best race finishes both came in 1991 with fourth in San Marino and Portugal. DOB: 23/4/61.

Grand Prix Record

Contested: 110   (1985-1994)
Victories: 0
Fastest laps: 0
Poles: 0

Year	Team	No.	Grand Prix
1985	Minardi Ford	2	Bra, Por
	Minardi MM Turbo	13	San, Can, USAE, Fra, GB, Ger, Aut, Hol, Ita, Bel, Eur, SA, Aus
1988	Minardi Ford	9	USAE (1), Fra, GB, Hun, Ita, Por, Esp, Jap, Aus
1989	Minardi Ford	15	Bra, San, Mon, Mex, USA, Can, Fra, GB (2), Ger, Hun, Bra, Ita, Por (2), Esp, Aus (1)
1990	Minardi Ford	15	USA, Bra, Mon, Can, Mex, Fra, GB, Ger, Hun, Bel, Ita, Por, Esp, Jap, Aus
1991	Minardi Ford	16	USA, Bra, San (3), Mon, Can, Mex, Fra, GB, Ger, Hun, Bel, Ita, Por (3), Esp, Jap, Aus

Year	Team	No.	Grand Prix
1992	Dallara Ferrari	16	SA, Mex, Bra, Esp (1), San (1), Mon, Can, Fra, GB, Ger, Hun, Bel, Ita, Por, Jap, Aus
1993	Minardi Ford	8	GB, Ger, Hun, Bel, Ita, Por, Jap, Aus
1994	Minardi Ford	16	Bra, Pac, San, Mon, Esp (2), Can, Fra (2), GB, Ger, Hun, Bel, Ita, Por, Eur, Jap, Aus

MONTERMINI, Andrea   Italy

Andrea Montermini failed to make his F1 debut in the Spanish Grand Prix at Jerez. As a replacement driver in Barcelona for Roland Ratzenberger, killed in practice at Imola, he crashed at 200kph, as the Simtek team watched in disbelief. He suffered broken bones in both legs and concussion. DOB: 30/5/64.

Grand Prix Record
Contested:	0
Victories:	0
Fastest laps:	0
Poles:	0

MORBIDELLI, Gianni   Italy

The first half of the 1994 season will easily be forgotten by this likeable Italian pictured opposite. He had yet to finish a race upto Germany, with the car failing him on six occasions and racing accidents taking him out on the other two. Things were to pick up though at Hockenheim as he followed team-mate Christian Fittipaldi home to take fifth place and his first two World Championship points for his new team. Sixth place was taken two races later in Belgium. He joined Arrows from Minardi for whom he had driven for just over two years. He made his debut in Brazil in 1990 for Dallara, and had driven one race for Ferrari at the end of the 1991 season where he had picked up his only top six finish prior to the 1994 season. DOB: 13/1/68.

Grand Prix Record
Contested:	50	(1990-1994)
Victories:	0	
Fastest laps:	0	
Poles:	0	

Year	Team	No.	Grand Prix
1990	Dallara Ford	1	Bra
	Minardi Ford	2	Jap, Aus

1991	Minardi Ferrari	15	USA, Bra, San, Mon, Can, Mex, Fra, GB, Ger, Hun, Bel, Ita, Por, Esp, Jap
	Ferrari	1	Aus (0.5)
1992	Minardi Lamborghini	15	SA, Mex, Bra, Esp, San, Mon, Can, Fra, GB, Ger, Bel, Ita, Por, Jap, Aus
1994	Footwork Ford	16	Bra, Pac, San, Mon, Esp, Can, Fra, GB, Ger (2), Hun, Bel (1), Ita, Por, Eur, Jap, Aus

NODA, Hideki   Japan

Hideki Noda drove for Simtek in the last three races of the 1994 season clocking up just 28 laps with three retirements. Technical problems took him out at Jerez and Adelaide, while he spun in front of his home fans at Suzuka. DOB: 7/3/69.

Grand Prix Record

Contested: 3   (1994)
Victories: 0
Fastest laps: 0
Poles: 0

Year	Team	No.	Grand Prix
1994	Larrousse Ford	3	Eur, Jap, Aus

PANIS, Olivier   France

Making his debut in the 1994 season, Olivier Panis was the most consistent driver of the year. He failed to finish in just the one race in front of his own fans in France. He finished the other fifteen although he was disqualified in Estoril. After the first corner pile up a Hockenheim, he showed immense maturity in taking his Ligier home in second place and added a further point in the next race in Hungary. His initial season in F1 was completed in Adelaide where he came home in fifth place. Not surprisingly, Ligier have resigned him for 1995. DOB: 2/9/64.

Grand Prix Record

Contested: 16   (1994)
Victories: 0
Fastest laps: 0
Poles: 0

Year Team	No.	Grand Prix
1994 Ligier Renault	16	Bra, Pac, San, Mon, Esp, Can, Fra, GB, Ger (6), Hun (1), Bel, Ita, Por, Eur, Jap, Aus (2)

RATZENBERGER, Roland   Austria

It was Roland Ratzenberger's dream to drive in F1. Unfortunately, the sport that he loved was to claim his life while he was qualifying for what would have been only his second Grand Prix. He signed for the new Simtek team and failed to qualify for the first race of the season in Brazil, but came home eleventh in Aida three weeks later. On the worst weekend in the history of the sport, Ratzenberger was killed in the second practice session for the San Marino Grand Prix at Imola. His car crashed into the wall just after the Villeneuve Curve at over 200 kph. DOB: 4/7/62. Died: 30/4/94.

Grand Prix Record

Contested: 1   (1994)
Victories: 0
Fastest laps: 0
Poles: 0

Year Team	No.	Grand Prix
1994 Simtek Ford	1	Pac

SALO, Mika   Finland

Mika Salo occupied the seat that no one else wanted in the final two races of the 1994 season. Most drivers were looking to other teams rather than Lotus for a drive, but Salo took a chance and came tenth in Japan before retiring in Australia. DOB: 30/11/66.

Grand Prix Record

Contested: 2   (1994)
Victories: 0
Fastest laps: 0
Poles: 0

Year	Team	No.	Grand Prix
1994	Lotus Mugen Honda	2	Jap, Aus

SCHIATTARELLA, Mimo   Italy

Mimmo Schiattarella drove for Simtek in Jerez and Australia at the end of 1994. He would also have raced in Japan had sponsorship not favoured Taki Inoue. He was the last of nineteen finishers in Spain and retired from the race in Adelaide with gearbox trouble. DOB: 17/11/67.

Grand Prix Record

Contested: 2
Victories: 0
Fastest laps: 0
Poles: 0

Year	Team	No.	Grand Prix
1994	Simtek Ford	2	Eur, Aus

SCHUMACHER, Michael   Germany

For all the problems he experienced, Michael Schumacher was generally regarded as the best F1 driver in 1994. Before all the trouble surrounding him and his Benetton blew up, he had won six of the opening seven Grand Prix and finished second in Spain where he showed the world just how good he was by driving for two-thirds of the race stuck in fifth gear. Schumacher was disqualified at Silverstone having finished second to Damon Hill after ignoring a black flag. He was later to be disqualified in Belgium for having an illegal skid block, and he was banned for two races after an unsuccessful appeal against the Silverstone incident. He returned from his ban to win at Jerez and finished second in Suzuka before the collision at Adelaide that gave him the Drivers' World Championship. Schumacher made his F1 debut with Jordan in Belgium in 1991 before moving to Benetton after just one race. His first win came in Belgium in 1992 and he followed this a year later with victory in Portugal. With the title under his belt, he'll be the one to beat in 1995. DOB: 3/1/69.

Grand Prix Record

Contested:	52	(1991-1994)
Victories:	10	1992 (Bel), 1993 (Por), 1994 (Bra, Pac, San, Can, Mon, Ger, Hun, Eur)
Fastest laps:	15	1992 (Bel, Aus), 1993 (Bra, Esp, Can, Fra, Ger), 1994 (Bra, Pac, Mon, Esp, Can, Hun, Eur, Aus)
Poles:	6	1994 (Mon, Esp, Can, Hun, Eur, Jap)

Year	Team	No.	Grand Prix
1991	Jordan Ford	1	Bel
	Benetton Ford	5	Ita (2), Por (1), Esp (1), Jap, Aus
1992	Benetton Ford	16	SA (3), Mex (4), Bra (4), Esp (6), San, Mon (3), Can (6), Fra, GB (3), Ger (4), Hun, Bel (10), Ita (4), Por, Jap, Aus (6)
1993	Benetton Ford	16	SA, Bra (4), Eur, San (6), Esp (4), Mon, Can (6), Fra (4), GB (6), Ger (6), Hun, Bel (6), Ita, Por (10), Jap, Aus
1994	Benetton Ford	14	Bra (10), Pac (10), San (10), Mon (10), Esp (6), Can (10), Fra (10), GB, Ger, Hun (10), Bel, Eur (10), Jap (6), Aus

SENNA (De Silva), Ayrton   Brazil

Ayrton Senna's death at Imola on May 1st 1994 made news the world over, but nowhere was the sense of disbelief felt more than in his home country of Brazil. The magnitude of the nations affection for their greatest ever sporting hero was shown by three days of national mourning and a state funeral attended by millions of normal people as well as the top names from the sport that claimed his life. Ayrton Senna had won three Drivers' World Championships with 41 victories from 161 grand prix. His move from McLaren to Williams at the start of the 1994 season had seen him take three straight pole positions but fail to finish a race. Following on from the death of Roland Ratzenberger the day before, it will take the sport a long time to overcome the events of that fateful weekend in San Marino. DOB: 21/3/60. Died:1/5/94.

Grand Prix Record

Contested: 161 (1984-1994)

Victories: 41 1985 (Por, Bel), 1986 (Esp, USAE), 1987 (Mon, USAE), 1988 (San, Can, USAE, GB, Ger, Hun, Bel, Jap), 1989 (San, Mon, Mex, Ger, Bel, Esp) 1990 (USA, Mon, Can, Ger, Bel, Ita), 1991 (USA, Bra, San, Mon, Hun, Bel, Aus), 1992 (Mon, Hun, Ita), 1993 (Bra, Eur, Mon, Jap, Aus).

Fastest laps: 19 1984 (Mon), 1985 (Por, Can, USAE), 1987 (Mon, USAE, Ita), 1988 (Mon, Can, Jap), 1989 (USA, Ger, Esp), 1990 (Mon, Ita), 1991 (Ita, Jap), 1992 (Por), 1993 (Eur)

Poles: 65 1985 (Por, San, Mon, USAE, Ita, Eur, Aus), 1986 (Bra, Esp, San, USAE, Fra, Hun, Por, Mex), 1987 (San), 1988 (Bra, San, Mon, Mex, Can, USAE, Ger, Hun, Bel, Ita, Esp, Jap, Aus), 1989 (Bra, San, Mon, Mex, USA, GB, Ger, Bel, Ita, Por, Esp, Jap, Aus), 1990 (Bra, San, Mon, Can, Ger, Bel, Ita, Esp, Jap, Aus), 1991 (USA, Bra, San, Mon, Hun, Bel, Ita, Aus), 1992 (Can), 1993 (Aus), 1994 (Bra, Pac, San).

Year	Team	No.	Grand Prix
1984	Toleman Hart Turbo	14	Bra, SA (1), Bel (1), Fra, Mon (6), Can, USAE, Dal, GB (4), Ger, Aut, Hol, Eur, Por (4)
1985	Lotus Renault Turbo	16	Bra, Por (9), San, Mon, Can, USAE, Fra, GB, Ger, Aut (6), Hol (4), Ita (4), Bel (9), Eur (6), SA, Aus
1986	Lotus Renault Turbo	16	Bra (6), Esp (9), San, Mon (4), Bel (6), Can (2), USAE (9), Fra, GB, Ger (6), Hun (6), Aut, Ita, Por (3), Mex (4), Aus
1987	Lotus Honda Turbo	16	Bra, San (6), Bel, Mon (9), USAE (9), Fra (3), GB (4), Ger (4), Hun (6), Aut (2), Ita (6), Por, Esp (2), Mex, Jap (6), Aus
1988	McLaren Honda Turbo	16	Bra, San (9), Mon, Mex (6), Can (9), USAE (9), Fra (6), GB (9), Ger (9), Hun (9), Bel (9), Ita, Por (1), Esp (3), Jap (9), Aus (6)
1989	McLaren Honda	16	Bra, San (9), Mon (9), Mex (9), USA, Can, Fra, GB, Ger (9), Hun (6), Bel (9), Ita, Por, Esp (9), Jap, Aus
1990	McLaren Honda	16	USA (9), Bra (4), San, Mon (9), Can (9), Mex, Fra (4), GB (4), Ger (9),

			Hun (6), Bel (9), Ita (9), Por (6), Esp, Jap, Aus
1991	McLaren Honda	16	USA (9), Bra (9), San (9), Mon (9), Can, Mex (4), Fra (4), GB (3), Ger, Hun (9), Bel (9), Ita (6), Por (6), Esp (2), Jap (6), Aus (9)
1992	McLaren Honda	16	SA (4), Mex, Bra, Esp, San (4), Mon (10), Can, Fra, GB, Ger (6), Hun (10), Bel (2), Ita (10), Por (4), Jap, Aus
1993	McLaren Ford	16	SA (6), Bra (10), Eur (10), San, Esp (6), Mon (10), Can, Fra (3), GB (2), Ger (3), Hun, Bel (3), Ita, Por, Jap (10), Aus (10)
1994	Williams Renault	3	Bra, Pac, San

SUZUKI, Aguri   Japan

Aguri Suzuki finished third in Japan for Lola, his best ever finish, in 1990. He drove for two years for Footwork in 1992 and 1993 failing to finish in the top six in that time. His only race last season was as a replacement for the suspended Eddie Irvine in the Jordan at the Pacific Grand Prix at Aida. DOB: 5/9/60.

Grand Prix Record

Contested: 59   (1988-1994)
Victories: 0
Fastest laps: 0
Poles: 0

Year	Team	No.	Grand Prix
1988	Lola Ford	1	Jap
1990	Lola Lamborghini	16	USA, Bra, San, Mon, Can, Mex, Fra, GB (1), Ger, Hun, Bel, Ita, Por, Esp (1), Jap (4), Aus
1991	Lola Ford	11	USA (1), San, Mon, Can, Mex, Fra, GB, Ger, Hun, Por, Jap
1992	Footwork Mugen	14	SA, Bra, Esp, San, Mon, Fra, GB, Ger, Hun, Bel, Ita, Por, Jap, Aus
1993	Footwork Mugen	16	SA, Bra, Eur, San, Esp, Mon, Can, Fra, GB, Ger, Hun, Bel, Ita, Por, Jap, Aus
1994	Jordan Hart	1	Pac

VERSTAPPEN, Jos   Holland

Jos Verstappen will be remembered for many years to come as the man in the Benetton that exploded into a fireball in the pit lane at Hockenheim. The incident immediately raised concerns over the safety of reintroducing refuelling. Verstappen responded well by taking successive podium finishes in the next two rounds, with third in both Hungary and Belgium. He took a further two points from a fifth place at Estoril to finish the season with ten World Championship points and 10th position in the Drivers' Championship. DOB: 4/3/72.

Grand Prix Record

Contested: 10   (1994)
Victories: 0
Fastest laps: 0
Poles: 0

Year	Team	No.	Grand Prix
1994	Benetton Ford	10	Bra, Pac, Fra, GB, Ger, Hun (4), Bel (4), Ita, Por (2), Eur

WENDLINGER, Karl   Austria

Karl Wendlinger was lucky. He lay in a coma for weeks following a horrific crash at Monaco, just two weeks after the deaths of Senna and Ratzenberger at Imola. As the picture below shows he received immediate track-side attention.

His season had promised so much, with sixth place in the Sauber in the opening race of the season at Interlagos and fourth at the San Marino Grand Prix. He was on the point of making a dramatic return to F1 at the end of the 1994 season, but changed his mind. The fourth place in San Marino equalled his best ever finish, in Canada with March in 1992 and a year later with Sauber in Italy. He made his F1 debut in 1991. DOB: 20/12/68.

Grand Prix Record

Contested: 35   (1991-1994)
Victories: 0
Fastest laps: 0
Poles: 0

Year	Team	No.	Grand Prix
1991	Leyton House Ilmor	2	Jap, Aus
1992	March Ilmor	14	SA, Mex, Bra, Esp, San, Mon, Can (3), Fra, GB, Ger, Hun, Bel, Ita, Por
1993	Sauber	16	SA, Bra, Eur, San, Esp, Mon, Can (1), Fra, GB, Ger, Hun (1), Bel, Ita (3), Por (2), Jap, Aus
1994	Sauber Mercedes	3	Bra (1), Pac, San (3)

ZANARDI, Alessandro   Italy

Alessandro Zanardi took over the second seat at Team Lotus from Pedro Lamy after four races of the 1994 season, but found the same frustration as team-mate Johnny Herbert. He could not add to his one points finish in Brazil in 1993, after he joined the Norfolk team after spells with Jordan and Minardi. DOB: 23/10/66.

Grand Prix Record

Contested: 25   (1991-1994)
Victories: 0
Fastest laps: 0
Poles: 0

Year	Team	No.	Grand Prix
1991	Jordan Ford	3	Esp, Jap, Aus
1992	Minardi Lamborghini	1	Ger
1993	Lotus Ford	11	SA, Bra (1), Eur, San, Esp, Mon, Can, Fra, GB, Ger, Hun
1994	Lotus Mugen Honda	10	Esp, Can, Fra, GB, Ger, Hun, Ita, Eur, Jap, Aus

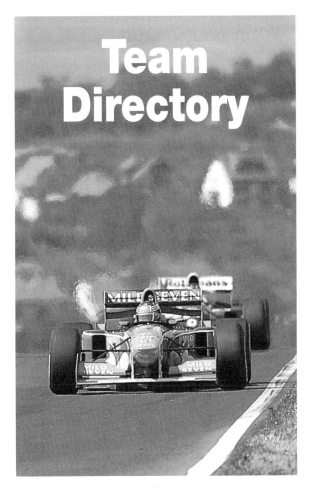

Team
Directory

Arrows

Arrows Grand Prix International
39 Barton Road, Water Eaton Industrial Estate, Bletchley, Bucks, MK2 3HW
Tel: +44 (0)1908 270047   Fax : +44 (0)1908 274123

Brief History

1977: Arrows Grand Prix founded. 1978: Riccardo Patrese scores Arrows' first point with sixth at Long Beach. Patrese takes second in Sweden – the team's best finish to date. Patrese banned for involvement in the accident that killed Ronnie Peterson. 1981: Patrese takes only pole position to date at Long Beach. 1984: Arrows switch to BMW Turbo engines. 1987: Megatron supply engines to Arrows after BMW pulls out. 1989: Arrows open new $10 million technical centre in Milton Keynes. 1989: Arrows are bought by Wataru Ohashi's Footwork Corporation. 1994: Jackie Oliver takes control after Footwork pull out.

Grand Prix Record

Contested:	255
Victories:	0
Pole Positions:	1
Fastest Laps:	1
Constructors' World Titles:	0 (Best: 4th 1988)
Drivers' World Championships:	0 (Best: =7th 1988)
Most Points in a Season:	23 (1988)
Total World Championship Points:	135

Review – Arrows suffer at hands of change

With the sponorship support of Footwork no longer available, the team reverted to the plain Arrows name for the start of the 1994 season with Gianni Morbidelli and Brazilian Christian Fittipaldi, nephew of the great Emerson, in the cockpits. The season looked to be making a promising start with Morbidelli taking sixth on the grid for the opening Grand Prix in Brazil. However, the team would only take just nine points all season as they struggled to come to terms with the technical changes forced upon the sport by the governing body following the events which were to unfold at Imola.

Fittipaldi – who had joined the team from Minardi – scored three points with fourth in Aida at the Pacific Grand Prix and he was excluded, having finished sixth in Montreal when his car was found to be underweight. Morbidelli was plagued by car problems as well as a couple of accidents in the first half of the season, and had to wait until the German Grand Prix, where he finished fifth behind team-mate Fittipaldi, to finish a race – and that only after both their cars had escaped the first corner pile-up. Spa in Belgium marked the last point of the season for the team as Morbidelli was promoted to sixth following the disqualification of Michael Schumacher.

The team's nine points secured them ninth place in the Constructors' World Championship for the sixth time in sixteen seasons.

The services of Gianni Morbidelli have been retained for the 1995 season but Christian Fittipaldi has been replaced by Japanese driver Taki Inoue who had just one outing last season for Simtek in his home Grand Prix where he survived just three laps before spinning out in torrential rain. Morbidelli always qualifed well, but was frequently outpaced by Fittipaldi on race day last season. The experience he has gained in his first season with Arrows, as well as with Minardi and a single outing with Ferrari, should see him drive the car to its maximum capability.

Arrows seemed to have found a competitive formula at the start of the 1994 season and hope that a chance to take stock of the new regulations will allow them to keep this edge during 1995.

Drivers and Results 1994

Driver	Country	Races	Pts	Psn	Com	Ret	F
Christian Fittipaldi	Brazil	16	6	=14th	9	6	0
Gianni Morbidelli	Italy	16	3	22nd	4	12	0

Grand Prix	Christian Fittipaldi	Gianni Morbidelli
Brazil	Retired	Retired
Pacific	4th	Retired
San Marino	Retired	Retired
Monaco	Retired	Retired
Spain	Retired	Retired
Canada	DQ	Retired
France	8th	Retired
Great Britain	9th	Retired
Germany	4th	5th
Hungary	14th	Retired
Belgium	Retired	6th
Italy	Retired	Retired
Portugal	8th	9th
Europe	17th	11th
Japan	8th	Retired
Australia	8th	Retired

Car Specifications 1995

Sponsors:	Unimat, Sasol, Techno Ferrari, Goodyear, Sergio Tacchini, Sparco, Matrix Design, Enkei, Alopex, Sally Ferries, Fiamm, Riccardo, Glasurit, Sika, Asia Magazine & Star TV
Owner:	Jackie Oliver
Designer:	Alan Jenkins
Team Manager:	Alan Harrison
Chief Mechanic:	Ken Fibley
Drivers :	Gianni Morbidelli & Taki Inoue

Engine:	**Hart**
Type:	V8
Spark Plugs:	Unipart
Electronics:	Tag
Fuel:	Sasol
Oil:	Sasol

Transmission:	**Arrows**
Gearbox:	6 speed semi-automatic
Gear Selection:	Arrows

Chassis

Dampers:	Arrrows	Tyres:	Goodyear
Brake Pads:	Brembo	Brake Discs:	Carbon Industrie
Brake Calipers:	Brembo	Radiators:	Secan
Steering:	Momo	Instruments:	PI Digital

Engines 1978-95

1978-83 – Ford. 1984-86 – BMW Turbo. 1987-88 – Megatron Turbo. 1989-90 – Ford Turbo. 1991 – Porsche. 1992-94 – Mugen-Honda. 1995 – Hart.

Drivers 1978-95

1978: R.Patrese. 1979: R.Patrese & J.Mass. 1980: R.Patrese & J.Mass. 1981: R.Patrese, S.Stohr & G.Villeneuve. 1982: M.Surer, M.Baldi & B.Henton. 1983: M.Surer, C.Serra, T.Boutsen. 1984: T.Boutsen, M.Surer. 1985: T.Boutsen & G.Berger. 1986: T.Boutsen, M.Sure & C.Danner. 1987: D.Warwick & E.Cheever. 1988: D.Warwick & E.Cheever. 1989: D.Warwick, E.Cheever & M.Donnelly. 1990: M.Alboreto & I.Capelli. 1991: M.Alboreto, A.Caffi & S.Johansson. 1992: M.Alboreto & A.Suzuki. 1993: D.Warwick & A.Suzuki. 1994: C.Fittipaldi & G.Morbidelli 1995: G.Morbidelli & T.Inoue.

Benetton

Benetton Formula Ltd
Whiteways Technical Centre, Enstone, Chipping Norton, Oxon, OX7 4EE
Tel: +44 (0)1608 678000   Fax: +44 (0)1608 678800

Brief History

1986: Benetton Formula One established after taking over the old Toleman team. 1987: Gerhard Berger wins in Mexico to give Benetton their first victory. 1990: Nelson Piquet leads home fellow Brazilian Roberto Moreno for first one-two. 1992: Michael Schumacher wins his first Grand Prix in Belgium. 1994: Michael Schumacher wins the Drivers' World Championship.

Grand Prix Record

Contested:	201
Victories:	15
Pole Positions:	9
Fastest Laps:	24
Drivers' World Championships:	1 (1994)
Constructors' World Championships:	0 (Best: 2nd 1994)
Most Points in a Season:	103 (1994)
Total World Championship Points:	526.5 points

Review – Controversy never far away

It was Michael Schumacher's year although his path to the 1994 Drivers' World Championship was hardly a smooth one with disqualifications, disputes and suspensions dogging his season as the Benetton team could seem to do no right in the eyes of the sport's governing body. That Schumacher prevailed and Benetton finished second in the Constructors' Championship said a great deal about their domination of the sport in 1994.

The season started in the best possible way with Schumacher winning five of the opening six Grand Prix and finishing second to Damon Hill in Spain after his car had become stuck in fifth gear after only a third of the race. The controversy though started at Silverstone in July.

After his sixth win in France, Schumacher overtook pole man Damon Hill on the parade lap at the Northamptonshire circuit in a perceived show of strength – but also an illegal manoeuvre. There are differing stories about what happened then but, that Schumacher was shown a black flag, and that he did not come into the pits cannot be denied – whatever the reasons. Schumacher claimed he had not seen the flag and his punishment from the governing body was a two-race ban. The German appealed at what was the start of a testing few months for the team as they encountered one problem after another. With Schumacher racing on under the threat of a ban if his appeal failed, the team were hit by more problems at the next race in Germany.

Whilst refuelling on a routine stop, Jos Verstappen's car went up in a ball of flames in the pit lane after petrol spilled over the hot engine. Verstappen and some of the mechanics suffered minor burns, but the team were hauled before the authorities to explain why a filter in the refuelling mechanism had been removed without permission. Despite the inevitable outcry Benetton walked away from the subsequent hearing unscathed.

After another Schumacher success in Hungary, Belgium was to cause more problems for Benetton. Following the deaths of Ayrton Senna and Roland Ratzenberger earlier in the season, a wooden skid-block had been placed under the car to reduce downforce by having to increase the height of the car. The 'plank' was 10mm thick and was allowed to reduce by a maximum of ten percent during a race. Schumacher was celebrating victory at Spa when officials announced his disqualification from the event because his wooden board measured only 7.4mm in places.

Schumacher's appeal against his two race ban failed, and with their main points scorer out of action and two wins for Damon Hill in Italy and Portugal, the lead in the Constructors' Championship was becoming as narrow as the Drivers' Championship. Schumacher returned in Jerez to win the European Grand Prix, and with points needed in the race for the Constructors' title, Johnny Herbert was drafted in from sister team Ligier in a bid for some points finishes. Herbert failed to finish in either Japan or Australia, and with Hill beating Schumacher in horrid conditions in Japan the title races went to the wire in Adelaide.

The collision between Schumacher and arch rival Damon Hill will be talked about as much if not more than the collision between Senna and Prost in Japan in 1989. Benetton lost out to Williams' in the Constructors' Championship, but Schumacher was Drivers' Champion. 1994 had not been a straightforward one for Benetton, but second place behind Williams and Schumacher World Champion certainly reads well with the promise of more to come.

For the 1995 season Benetton have stuck with the driver combination that ended 1994 with Johnny Herbert supporting the Drivers' World Champion in the team for which he made his Grand Prix debut. There is a change though with Renault supplying the engine after the reliable Ford model was ditched.

Driver	Country	Races	Pts	Psn	Com	Ret	F
Michael Schumacher	Germany	14	92	1st	10	2	0
Jos Verstappen	Holland	10	10	10th	4	6	0
JJ Lehto*	Finland	6	1	=25th	3	3	0
Johnny Herbert†	Great Britain	2	0	–	0	2	0

* Lehto also had two races for Sauber. † Herbert also had 13 races for Lotus and one race for Ligier.

Grand Prix	Schumacher	Verstappen	Lehto	Herbert
Brazil	1st	Retired	–	–
Pacific	1st	Retired	–	–
San Marino	1st	–	Retired	–
Monaco	1st	–	7th	–
Spain	2nd	–	Retired	–
Canada	1st	–	6th	–
France	1st	–	–	–
Great Britain	DQ	8th	–	–
Germany	Retired	Retired	–	–
Hungary	1st	3rd	–	–
Belgium	DQ	3rd	–	–
Italy	–	Retired	9th	–
Portugal	–	5th	Retired	–
Europe	1st	Retired	–	–
Japan	2nd	–	–	Retired
Australia	Retired	–	–	Retired

Car Specifications 1995

Sponsors:	Mild Seven, Benetton Sportsystem, Renault, Bitburger, Elf
Owner:	Flavio Briatore
Designer:	Ross Brown
Team Manager:	Joan Villadelprat
Chief Mechanic:	Mick Alnsley-Cowlishaw
Drivers:	Michael Schumacher, Jonny Herbert
Test Driver:	Jos Verstappen

Engine: **Renault**
Type:	RS07
Cylinders:	10 – four valves per cylinder
Fuel:	Elf
Oil:	Elf

Transmission: **Benetton**
Gearbox:	Six Speed
Clutch:	AP

Dimensions

Overall Length:	4500mm	Wheelbase:	2800mm
Front Track:	1690mm	Rear Track:	1618mm
Height:	950mm		

Chassis

Front Suspension:	Pushrod	Rear Suspension:	Pushrod
Tyres:	Goodyear	Brake Discs:	Brembo
Brake Pads:	Brembo		
Brake Calipers:	Brembo		
Radiators:	Water		
Cooling:	Separate water and oil		

Engines 1981-95

(1981-85 – Toleman). 1981-85 – Hart Turbo. 1986 – BMW Turbo. 1987 – Ford Turbo. 1988-94 – Ford. 1995 – Renault.

Drivers 1981-95

1981:B.Henton & D.Warwick. 1982: D.Warwick & T.Fabi. 1983: D.Warwick & B.Giacomelli. 1984: A.Senna, J.Cecotto, S.Johansson & P.Martini. 1985: T.Fabi & P.Ghinzani. 1986: T.Fabi & G.Berger. 1987: T.Boutsen & T.Fabi. 1988: A.Nannini & T.Boutsen. 1989: A.Nannini, J.Herbert & E.Pirro. 1990: A.Nannini, N.Piquet & R.Moreno. 1991: N.Piquet, R.Moreno & M.Schumacher. 1992: M.Schumacher & M.Brundle. 1993: M.Schumacher & R.Patrese. 1994: M.Schumacher, J.Verstappen, JJ Lehto & J.Herbert. 1995: M.Schumacher & J.Herbert. *NB: Team name Toleman 81-85.*

Ferrari

Ferrari
Via Ascari 55-57, 41053 Maranello (Mo), Italy
Tel: +39 536 941161/1188   Fax: +39 536 946488

Brief History

1898: Enzo Ferrari born in Modena, Italy. 1929: Enzo Ferrari forms his company. 1947: Franco Cortese wins the Grand Prix of Rome to record Ferrari's first race win. 1951: Jose Gonzalez records Ferrari's first Formula One victory. 1952: Alberto Ascari wins the Drivers' World Championship in a Ferrari. 1953: Ascari wins back-to-back titles driving for the Modena based team. 1956: Juan-Manuel Fangio wins World Championship with Ferrari.

1958: Mike Hawthorn becomes the third Ferrari driver to win the title. 1961: Phil Hill leads Ferrari to the 'double' of both Drivers' and Constructors' titles. 1964: John Surtees takes the World Championship in a Ferrari. 1969: Lowest ever Ferrari score of 7 points achieved in Constructors' World Championship. 1975: Niki Lauda takes title in a Ferrari ahead of Emerson Fittipaldi. 1977: Lauda repeats his success of two years earlier. 1979: Jody Scheckter wins his only World Championship driving a Ferrari. 1983: Ferrari win the last of their eight World Constructors' Championships.

Grand Prix Record

Contested:	537
Victories:	104
Pole Positions:	113
Fastest Laps:	119
Constructors' World Titles:	8
Drivers' World Championships:	7
Most Points in a Season:	113 (1979)
Total World Championship Points:	1804.5

Review – Power not subtle enough

During 1994 Ferrari maintained their recent consistency with third place behind Williams and Benetton in the Constructors' Championship, and with Gerhard Berger and Jean Alesi third and fifth respectively in the Drivers' Championship. Nicola Larini was equal fourteenth from just two starts when he was called in to replace an injured Alesi, his six points coming from second place in the ill-fated San Marino Grand Prix at Imola.

The Ferrari team had produced one of the most powerful engines of all the teams but it proved not to be well suited to the more subtle circuits and indeed, the only track where it proved to be a real advantage was Hockenheim with Berger and Alesi on the front row of the grid – the Austrian going on to take Ferrari's only win of the season. Berger added to this with second in Aida, Monza and Adelaide with third placing in Monaco and France as well as taking pole in Portugal. Alesi took pole in Italy and finished second at Silverstone and third in Brazil, Canada and Japan. Reliability also proved to be a thorn in the Ferrari side with no less than 14 retirements from 32 starts.

Ferrari have gained more than 5,000 victories in motor sport the world over, with Berger's win in Germany last year their 104th in Formula One – a record that the Italian team share with rivals McLaren. Berger and Alesi are paired together once again for the 1995 season, and with an improved and more reliable car they can mount a strong challenge for both titles once again.

Drivers and Results 1994

Driver	Country	Races	Pts	Psn	Com	Ret	F
Jean Alesi	France	14	24	5th	8	6	0
Gerhard Berger	Austria	16	41	3rd	9	7	0
Nicola Larini	Italy	2	6	=14th	1	1	0

Grand Prix	Jean Alesi	Gerhard Berger	Nicola Larini
Brazil	3rd	Retired	–
Pacific	–	2nd	Retired
San Marino	–	Retired	2nd
Monaco	5th	3rd	–
Spain	4th	Retired	–
Canada	3rd	4th	–
France	Retired	3rd	–
Great Britain	2nd	Retired	–
Germany	Retired	1st	–
Hungary	Retired	12th	–
Belgium	Retired	Retired	–
Italy	Retired	2nd	–
Portugal	Retired	Retired	–
Europe	10th	5th	–
Japan	3rd	Retired	–
Australia	6th	2nd	–

Car Specifications 1995

Sponsors:	Marlboro, Agip, Pioneer, Telecom Italia, Fiat, Magneti Marelli, SKF, Brembo, Arexons, Momo, TRW & Sabelt
Chairman:	Luca Di Montezemolo
Designers:	John Bernard (chassis) & Paolo Martinelli (engine)
Team Manager:	Jean Todt
Chief Mechanic:	Nigel Stepney
Drivers:	Jean Alesi & Gerhard Berger
Test Driver:	Nicola Larini

Engine: **Ferrari**

Type:	044/1
Cylinders:	12
Injection:	Magnetti Marelli
Spark Plugs:	Champion
Electronics:	Magnetti Marelli
Fuel:	Agip
Oil:	Agip

Transmission: **Ferrari**
Gearbox: Transverse sequential 6 speed & reverse
Clutch: Manual command on steering wheel

Dimensions

Overall Length:	4380mm	Wheelbase:	2915mm
Front Track:	1690mm	Rear Track:	1605mm
Overall Width:	1995mm	Height:	980mm

Chassis

Front Suspension:	Push-Rod	Rear Suspension:	Push-Rod
Dampers:	Ferrari	Tyres:	Goodyear
Brake Pads:	Brembo	Brake Calipers:	Brembo
Steering:	Momo	Instruments:	Magnetti Marelli

Wheel Diameter (Front/Rear): 13" & 13"
Wheel Rim Widths (Front/Rear): 11.7" & 13.75"

Engines 1950-95

1950-80 – Ferrari. 1981-88 – Ferrari Turbo. 1989-95 – Ferrari.

Drivers 1950-94

1950: A.Ascari, L.Villoresi, R.Sommer, D.Serafini, P.Whitehead. 1951: A.Ascari, L.Villoresi, J.Gonzalez, P.Taruffi. 1952: A.Ascari, G.Farina, L.Villoresi, P.Taruffi, P.Whitehead. 1953: A.Ascari, G.Farina, L.Villoresi, M.Hawthorn. 1954: G.Farina, J.Gonzalez, M.Hawthorn, U.Maglioli, M.Trintignant, R.Manzon. 1955: M.Hawthorn, M.Trintignant, G.Farina, U.Maglioli & J.Gonzalez. 1956: J.Fangio, P.Collins, E.Castelotti, L.Musso, O.Gendibien, A.de Portigo & M.Trintignant. 1957: P.Collins, M.Hawthorn, L.Musso, M.Trintignant, C.Perdisa, E.Castellotti, A.de Portigo & W.Von Trips. 1958: M.Hawthorn, P.Collins, L.Musso, W.Von Trips, P.Hill & O.Gendibien. 1959: T.Brooks, P.Hill, J.Behra, D.Gurney, C.Allison & O.Gendibien. 1960: P.Hill, W.Von Trips, R.Ginther, C.Allison & W.Mairesse. 1961: P.Hill, W.Von Trips, R.Ginther, G.Baghetti & W.Mairesse. 1962: P.Hill, W.Mairesse, G.Baghetti, L.Bandini & R.Rodriguez. 1963: W.Mairesse, J.Surtees, L.Bandini & L.Scarfiotti. 1964: J.Surtees & L.Bandini. 1965: J.Surtees & L.Bandini. 1966: J.Surtees, L.Bandini, M.Parkes & L.Scarfiotti. 1967: L.Bandini, C.Amon, M.Parkes & L.Scarfiotti. 1968: J.Ickx, C.Amon & A.de Adamich. 1969: C.Amon & P.Rodriguez. 1970: J.Ickx, I.Giunti & C.Regazzoni. 1971: J.Ickx, C.Regazzoni & M.Andretti. 1972: J.Ickx, C.Regazzoni & M.Andretti. 1973: J.Ickx & A.Merzario. 1974: C.Regazzoni & N.Lauda. 1975: C.Regazzoni & N.Lauda. 1976: N.Lauda, C.Regazzoni & C.Reutemann. 1977: N.Lauda, C.Reutemann & G.Villeneuve. 1978: C.Reutemann & G.Villeneuve. 1979: J.Scheckter & G.Villeneuve. 1980: J.Scheckter & G.Villeneuve. 1981: G.Villeneuve & D.Pironi. 1982: G.Villeneuve, D.Pironi, P.Tambay & M.Andretti. 1983:

P.Tambay & R.Arnoux. 1984: M.Alboreto & R.Arnoux. 1985: M.Alboreto, R.Arnoux & S.Johansson. 1986: M.Alboreto & S.Johansson. 1987: M. Alboreto & G.Berger. 1988: M.Alboreto & G.Berger. 1989: N.Mansell & G.Berger. 1990: A.Prost & N.Mansell. 1991: A.Prost, J.Alesi & G.Morbidelli. 1992: J.Alesi, I.Capelli & N.Larini. 1993: J.Alesi & G.Berger. 1994: J.Alesi, G.Berger & N.Larini. 1995: J.Alesi & G.Berger.

Forti

Forti Formula One
Via Luigi Einaudi 33, Allessandria, Italy.
Tel: +39 131 246890   Fax: +39 131 246891

Grand Prix Record

Contested: 0
Victories: 0
Pole Positions: 0
Fastest Laps: 0
Constructors' World Championships: 0
Drivers' World Championships: 0
Most Points in a Season: 0
Total World Championship Points: 0

Review – New in town

The only new team in 1995, Forti enter Formula One with a good recent pedigree in Formula 3000 and have the financial backing in the shape of 17 million dollars from Parmalat who are returning to F1 ten years after their successful partnership with Brabham. What is not known is how they will adapt to the huge step up to Formula One, but they have the benefit of a Ford Cosworth engine. Pedro Diniz has the ability to go fast but has a reputation for crashing out – hardly a qualification for competing at the top.

Engine 1995

1995 – Ford

Drivers 1995

1995: P.Diniz & R.Moreno*
Initially for first two Grand Prix only.

Jordan

Jordan Grand Prix Ltd
Buckingham Road, Silverstone, Northants, NN12 8JT
Tel: +44 (0)1327 857153   Fax: +44 (0)1327 858120

Brief History

1980: Eddie Jordan forms Jordan Motor Racing Team. 1987: Johnny Herbert wins British Formula 3 Championship driving a Jordan. 1988: Jean Alesi takes the International F3000 title for Jordan. 1990: Jordan F1 formed. 1991: Jordan scored their first F1 points with Andrea de Cesaris fourth in Canada. 1993: Jordan sign a deal to use Hart engines until the end of the 1994 season.

Grand Prix Record

Contested:	60
Victories:	0
Pole Positions:	1
Fastest Laps:	1
Constructors' World Championships:	0 (Best: 5th 1994)
Drivers' World Championships:	0 (Best: 6th 1994)
Most Points in a Season:	28 (1994)
Total World Championship Points:	45

Review – Jordan progress continues

The partnership of Barrichello and Irvine has been retained for the 1995 season and they rewarded the team with the largest points total to date in the Constuctors' World Championship. For Barrichello the season started and ended well with fourth in the opening race at Interlagos followed up at the Pacific Grand Prix at Aida with the team's first podium finish as he came home in third place. After fourth place at Silverstone in July, he took nine points in the final five races of the season with fourth in Italy, Portugal and Australia to finish sixth in the Drivers' World Championship with 19 points.

Eddie Irvine's season was put on temporray hold immediately after the opening round in Brazil. Irvine, who had picked up a reputation for aggressive driving in his only two Grand Prix drives prior to the start of the 1994 season, was banned for one race after he was blamed for a four car pile up at Interlagos. He took the decision to appeal, only for the ban to be increased to three races, so he was forced to sit out in Aida, San Marino and Monaco.

Aguri Suzuki retired in the Pacific Grand Prix, with Andrea de Cesaris failing to impress in Imola before picking up three points for fourth in Monte Carlo. Irvine returned to pick up a single point at the Spanish Grand Prix in Barcelona but had to wait until the end of the season for his best results with fourth at Jerez and fifth at Suzuka for 16th in the Drivers' Championship with six points.

In 1994 Jordan set a standard that they will hope to improve upon. Eddie Jordan has seen his team progress each year for the past fourteen since they were formed, and 1995 should be no exception. They have maintained their exciting driver line-up of Barrichello and Irvine for the new season and the only difference this year will come from the switch to the Peugeot V10 engine. The French engine suppliers have had a year with McLaren to come to terms with Formula One and Jordan will certainly be hoping for greater reliability than was shown last season. Although they lack the cool head of an experienced driver in their line-up, the combination of the Brazilian and the Ulsterman gives Jordan a psychological lift that is not present in any other team. If the engine proves reliable and one of the top teams has a bad year, Jordan could well sneak into the top four teams.

Drivers and Results 1994

Driver	Country	Races	Pts	Psn	Com	Ret	F
Rubens Barrichello	Brazil	16	19	6th	8	7	1
Eddie Irvine	Great Britain	13	6	=14th	5	8	1
Aguri Suzuki	Japan	1	–	–	0	1	0
Andrea de Cesaris*	Italy	2	4	=18th	1	1	0

*de Cesaris also had nine races and scored one point for Sauber.

Grand Prix	Barrichello	Irvine	Suzuki	de Cesaris
Brazil	4th	Retired	–	–
Pacific	3rd	–	Retired	–
San Marino	NS	–	–	Retired
Monaco	Retired	–	–	4th
Spain	Retired	6th	–	–
Canada	7th	Retired	–	–
France	Retired	Retired	–	–
Great Britain	4th	Retired	–	–
Germany	Retired	Retired	–	–
Hungary	Retired	Retired	–	–
Belgium	Retired	13th	–	–
Italy	4th	Retired	–	–
Portugal	4th	7th	–	–
Europe	12th	4th	–	–
Japan	Retired	5th	–	–
Australia	4th	Retired	–	–

Car Specifications 1995

Sponsors:	Total, Marlboro, Ape, Best, Cadtek, Control Techniques, Diavia, Fiamm, Fujitsu ICL, Glasurit, Goodyear, Fanghi d'alga Guam, IBSV, Ireland, Kibon, Kremlyovskaya Vodka, Motorscan, Osma, OZ Wheels, Pepsi, Pizza Hut, Polti, Rockport, Ruffles, Scania, Sally Freight, Sparco, Uliveto, Unipart.
Owner:	Eddie Jordan
Designer:	Gary Anderson
Team Manager:	John Walton
Chief Mechanic:	Paul Thompson
Drivers:	Rubens Barrichello & Eddie Irvine

Engine: **Peugeot**

Type:	A10
Cylinders:	10
Injection:	Peugeot
Spark Plugs:	NGK
Electronics:	TAG
Fuel:	TOTAL
Oil:	TOTAL

Transmission: **Jordan**

Gearbox:	Jordan 7 Speed & Reverse
Gear Selection:	Hewland
Drive Shafts:	Jordan
Clutch:	Twin Plate Tilton

Dimensions

Overall Length:	4450mm	Wheelbase:	2950mm
Front Track:	1700mm	Rear Track:	1618mm
Overall Width:	2000mm	Height:	950mm

Chassis

Front Suspension:	Jordan	Rear Suspension:	Jordan
Dampers:	Jordan	Tyres:	Goodyear
Brake Pads:	SEP	Brake Discs:	SEP
Steering:	Rack & Pinion	Radiators:	Secan
Brake Calipers:	Brembo 4 Piston Metal Matrix		

Wheel Diameter (Front/Rear): 13" & 13"
Wheel Rim Widths (Front/Rear): 11.75" & 13.75"

Engines 1991-95

1991 – Ford. 1992 – Yamaha. 1993-94 – Hart. 1995 – Peugeot.

Drivers 1991-95

1991: A.de Cesaris, B.Gachot, R.Moreno, M.Schumacher & A.Zanardi. 1992: S.Modena & M.Gugelmin. 1993: R.Barrichello, I.Capelli, T.Boutsen, M.Apicella, E.Nespatti & E.Irvine. 1994: R.Barrichello, E.Irvine, A.Suzuki & A.de Cesaris. 1995: R.Barrichello & E.Irvine.

Larrousse

Larrousse F1
Z.E. de Signes, B.P. 702-83030, Toulon, Cedex 9, France
Tel: +33 943 28888   Fax: +33 943 28141

Brief History

1992: Larrousse make their F1 debut in the first race of the season in South Africa. Bertrand Gachot takes his first point with sixth in Monaco. 1993: Larrousse take only three points during their second season.

Grand Prix Record

Contested:	48
Victories:	0
Pole Positions:	0
Fastest Laps:	0
Constructors' World Championships:	0 (Best: =10th 1993)
Drivers' World Championships:	0 (Best: =11th 1993)
Most Points in a Season:	3 (1993)
Total World Championship Points:	6

Review – Cashing in

The 1994 season saw Larrousse repeat the two top sixth finishes of the previous year with Erik Comas sixth at Aida for the Pacific Grand Prix and again at Hockenheim. Comas competed in all but the last race of the season in Adelaide as the team struggled financially towards the end of the year with the second car occupied by Olivier Beretta, Philippe Alliot, Yannick Dalmas and Hideki Noda – bringing the total number of drivers to six, more than any other rival team. Hideki Noda's three races all ended in retirement.

Jean-Denis Deletraz came up with enough money to replace Comas in the Australian Grand Prix. With the financial demands of Formula One coupled with Larrousse's lack of resources they will do well to maintain their 1994 results through 1995.

Drivers and Results 1994

Driver	Country	Races	Pts	Psn	Com	Ret	F
Erik Comas	France	15	2	23rd	7	8	0
Olivier Berreta	Italy	10	–	–	4	6	0
Philippe Alliot*	France	1	–	–	0	1	0
Yannick Dalmas	France	2	–	–	1	1	0
Hideki Noda	Japan	3	–	–	0	3	0
Jean-Denis Deletraz	France	1	–	–	0	1	0

Alliot also had one race for McLaren.

Grand Prix	Comas	Berreta	Alliot	Dalmas	Hoda
Brazil	9th	Retired	–	–	–
Pacific	6th	Retired	–	–	–
San Marino	Retired	Retired	–	–	–
Monaco	10th	8th	–	–	–
Spain	Retired	Retired	–	–	–
Canada	Retired	Retired	–	–	–
France	Retired	Retired	–	–	–
Great Britain	Retired	14th	–	–	–
Germany	6th	7th	–	–	–
Hungary	8th	9th	–	–	–
Belgium	Retired	–	Retired	–	–
Italy	8th	–	–	Retired	–
Portugal	Retired	–	–	14th	–
Europe	Retired	–	–	–	Retired
Japan	9th	–	–	–	Retired
Australia*	–	–	–	–	Retired

Jean-Denis Deletraz drove in the Australian Grand Prix (Retired)

Engines 1992-95

1992-94 – Lamborghini. 1994-95 – Ford.

Drivers 1992-95

1992: B.Gachot & U.Katayama. 1993: P.Alliot, E.Comas & T.Suzuki. 1994: O.Beretta, E.Comas, P.Alliot, Y.Dalmas, H.Noda & J-D Deletraz. 1995: C.Bouchut & E.Helary.

Ligier

Ligier Formule 1
Technopole – 58470, Magny-Cours, France
Tel: +33 866 06200   Fax: +33 862 12296

Brief History

1976: Ligier enter F1 at the end of the 1976 season. Jacques Laffite takes pole and sets the fastest lap in Italy. 1979: Laffite wins the opening two Grand Prix in Argentina and Brazil. 1980: Ligier finish second in the Constructors' World Championship behind Williams. 1983: Ligier fail to score a point in the season for the first time in their history.

Grand Prix Record

Contested:	293
Victories:	8
Pole Positions:	9
Fastest Laps:	11
Constructors' World Championships:	0 (Best: 2nd in 1980)
Drivers' World Championships:	0 (Best: 4th 1979, 1980, 1981)
Most Points in a Season:	66 (1980)
Total World Championship Points:	349

Review – Double not enough to impress

The 1994 season saw the team achieve its best ever two car finish in a Grand Prix, but despite the ten points scored in Germany only seventh place with 13 points in the Constructors' World Championship could be obtained. The race at Hockenheim was interesting to say the least with Olivier Panis, in his first season in the sport, leading home team-mate Eric Bernard behind the Ferrari of Gerhard Berger. Cynics will point to the fact that the points would not have been scored had eleven cars not crashed out at the first corner, but with their cars clear of the pile-up, they were not heard to argue on the side of having the race stopped.

Panis was their most consistent driver of 1994 finishing all but one race, and along with his second placing in Germany he picked up sixth in Hungary and fifth in the last race of the season in Australia. Bernard did nothing else apart from drive around a deserted Hockenheim in late July before switching to Lotus as Johnny Herbert came in the opposite direction for just the one race before joining Benetton. Franck Lagorce drove and retired, in the final two races of the season.

Martin Brundle returns for 1995 after a year with McLaren to partner Olivier Panis, and it will need a driver of the calibre of Brundle if Ligier are to improve on their 13 points of last year. The input from the Benetton take-over showed some signs towards the latter part of last year, but it must be very doubtful if it will have any impact in the immediate future.

Drivers and Results 1994

Driver	Country	Races	Pts	Psn	Com	Ret	F
Eric Bernard*	France	143	4	=18th	10	3	0
Olivier Panis	France	16	9	11th	14	1	1
Johnny Herbert†	Great Britain	1	–	–	1	0	0
Franck Lagorce	France	2	–	–	0	2	0

Bernard also had one race for Lotus. † Herbert also had 13 races for Lotus and two for Benetton.

Grand Prix	Bernard	Panis	Herbert	Lagorce
Brazil	Retired	11th	–	–
Pacific	10th	9th	–	–
San Marino	12th	11th	–	–
Monaco	Retired	9th	–	–
Spain	8th	7th	–	–
Canada	13th	12th	–	–
France	Retired	Retired	–	–
Great Britain	13th	12th	–	–
Germany	3rd	2nd	–	–
Hungary	10th	6th	–	–
Belgium	10th	7th	–	–
Italy	7th	10th	–	–
Portugal	10th	FQ	–	–
Europe	–	9th	8th	–
Japan	–	11th	–	Retired
Australia	–	5th	–	Retired

Car Specifications 1995

Sponsors:	Gitanes, Elf
Owner:	Flavio Briatore
Designer:	Frank Dernie
Team Manager:	Cesare Fiorio
Drivers:	Martin Brundle, Aguri Suzuki & Olivier Panis
Test Driver:	Franck Lagorce

Engine:	**Mugen Honda**		
Type:	V10 MF-301H		
Cylinders:	10 - 4 valves per cylinder		
Injection:	Honda PGM-F1		
Fuel:	ATL rubber fuel cell		
Oil:	Elf lubricants in 8-litre capacity tank		
Cooling:	Separate water radiators in each side pod and one water/oil exchanger on right-hand side of engine.		

Transmission:

Gearbox:	Transverse six-speed
Gear Selection:	Semi-automatic

Dimensions

Overall Length:	4335mm	Wheelbase:	2935mm
Front Track:	1693mm	Rear Track:	1608mm
Overall Width:	1995mm	Height:	950mm

Chassis

Front Suspension:	Push-Rod	Rear Suspension:	Push-Rod
Dampers:	Ligier	Tyres:	Goodyear
Brake Pads:	Brembo	Brake Discs:	Brembo
Brake Calipers:	Brembo one-piece		

Engines (1976-95)

1978-78 – Matra. 1979-80 – Ford. 1981-84 – Matra. 1984-86 – Renault Turbo. 1987 – Megatron Turbo. 1988 – Judd. 1989-90 – Ford. 1991 – Lamborghini. 1992-94 – Renault. 1995 – Mugen-Honda.

Drivers 1976–95

1976: J.Laffite. 1977: J.Laffite. 1978: J.Laffite. 1979: J.Laffite, P.Delailler & J.Ickx. 1980: J.Laffite & D.Pironi. 1981: J.Laffite, J-P Jarier, J-P Jabouille & P.Tambay. 1982: J.Laffite & E.Cheever. 1983: J-P Jarier & R.Boesel. 1984: A.de Cesaris & F.Hesnault. 1985: J.Laffite, A.de Cesaris & P.Streiff. 1986: R.Arnoux, J.Laffite & P.Alliot. 1987: R.Arnoux & P.Ghinzani. 1988: R.Arnoux & S.Johansson. 1989: R.Arnoux & O.Grouillard. 1990: P.Alliot & N.Larini. 1991: T.Boutsen & E.Comas. 1992: T.Boutsen & E.Comas. 1993: M.Brundle & M.Blundell. 1994: E.Bernard, O.Panis, J.Herbert & F.Lagorce. 1995: M.Brundle, A.Suzuki & O.Panis.

McLaren

McLaren International Ltd
Unit 22, Woking Business Park, Albert Drive, Woking, Surrey, GU21 5JY
Tel: +44 (0)1483 728211   Fax: +44 (0)1483 720157

Brief History

1959: Bruce McLaren makes his F1 debut driving for the Cooper works team.
1963: Bruce McLaren Motor Racing Ltd founded. 1966: McLaren make their
Grand Prix debut at Monaco. 1968: Bruce McLaren wins in Belgium for his
own team's first F1 victory. McLaren finish second behind Lotus in
Constructors' World Championship. 1970: Bruce McLaren killed at
Goodwood whilst testing a CanAm sportscar. 1973: Emerson Fittipaldi leads
McLaren to the Drivers' & Constructors' Championship double. 1976: James
Hunt takes the Drivers' World Championship by a point from Niki Lauda.
1984: Niki Lauda beats team-mate Alain Prost by just half a point to take the
Drivers' title. 1985: Alan Prost takes the title ahead of Michele Alboreto.
1986: Prost retains his title after Nigel Mansell goes out in the final race at
Adelaide. 1988: Senna takes the title by three points from Prost. McLaren
post a record Constructors' Championship score of 199 points. 1989: Prost
takes the title from Senna by 16 points for another McLaren 'double'. 1990:
Senna regains the title from Prost by seven points. 1991: Senna wins his third
World Drivers' Championship.

Grand Prix Record

Contested:	410
Victories:	104
Pole Position:	79
Fastest Laps:	69
Constructors' World Championships:	7
Drivers' World Championships:	8
Most Points in a Season:	199 (1988)
Total World Championship Points:	1865.5

Review – Low ebb in difficult season

Last season was a difficult one for McLaren. They started with a car that they
knew could not compete at the very highest level and they took an enormous
gamble by using a Peugeot engine that nobody knew much about. Their
points total of 42 in the Constructors' Championship was their lowest for over

a decade with Finland's Mika Hakkinen fourth in the Drivers' Championship with 26 and England's Martin Brundle seventh with 16.

Hakkinen picked up a one race ban for his involvement in the first corner pile-up at the German Grand Prix in Hockenheim, but returned from missing the race in Hungary to record second in Belgium and a hat-trick of third in Italy, Portugal and Europe to add to four point podium finishes in San Marino and Britain. Brundle also managed a second place finish in Monaco and was third in the final race of the season in Australia.

The 1995 season also looks set to be a difficult one for McLaren. They have replaced the Peugeot engine in preference to a new Mercedes V10 but this may not be enough for an improved performance all round as although the engine took the blame for a great deal that did not go right last season, it was be no means the only factor. McLaren can take heart from the coup of signing Nigel Mansell to the team to partner Hakkinen for 1995 and that can only help the cause.

Drivers and Results 1994

Driver	Country	Races	Pts	Psn	Com	Ret	F
Mika Hakkinen	Finland	15	26	4th	8	7	0
Martin Brundle	Great Britain	16	16	7th	6	10	0
Philippe Alliot*	France	1	–	–	0	1	0

* Alliot also had one race for Larrousse.

Grand Prix	Mika Hakkinen	Martin Brundle	Philippe Alliot
Brazil	Retired	Retired	–
Pacific	Retired	Retired	–
San Marino	3rd	8th	–
Monaco	Retired	2nd	–
Spain	Retired	Retired	–
Canada	Retired	Retired	–
France	Retired	Retired	–
Great Britain	3rd	Retired	–
Germany	Retired	Retired	–
Hungary	–	4th	Retired
Belgium	2nd	Retired	–
Italy	3rd	6th	–
Portugal	3rd	2nd	–
Europe	3rd	Retired	–
Japan	7th	Retired	–
Australia	12th	3rd	–

Car Specifications 1995

Sponsors:	Marlboro, TAG, NGK, AP Racing, Mobil, Bilstein
Team Principal:	Ron Dennis
Designer:	Neil Oatley (chassis) & Mario Illien (engine)
Team Manager:	Dave Ryan
Chief Mechanic:	Paul Simpson
Drivers:	Nigel Mansell/Mark Blundell & Mike Hakkinen

Engine:	**Mercedes-Benz**
Type:	F0110
Cylinders:	10
Injection:	TAG
Spark Plugs:	NGK
Electronics:	TAG
Fuel:	Mobil
Oil:	Mobil

Transmission:	**McLaren**
Gearbox:	6 speed semi-automatic
Gear Selection:	McLaren
Drive Shafts:	McLaren
Clutch:	McLaren

Chassis

Dampers:	Bilstein	Tyres:	Goodyear
Brake Pads:	AP Racing	Brake Discs:	AP Racing
Brake Calipers:	AP Racing		
Radiators:	McLaren/Calsonic		

Engines 1966-95

1966-82 – Ford. 1983-87 – TAG-Porsche Turbo. 1988 – Honda Turbo. 1989-92 – Honda. 1993 - Ford. 1994 – Peugeot. 1995 – Mercedes.

Drivers 1966-95

1966: B.McLaren. 1967: B.McLaren. 1968: D.Hulme & D.Gurney. 1969: B.McLaren, D.Hulme & V.Elford. 1970: B.McLaren, D.Hulme, D.Gurney & J.Surtees. 1971: D.Hulme, P.Gethin & J.Oliver. 1972: D.Hulme & P.Revson 1973: D.Hulme, P.Revson, J.Scheckter. 1974: E.Fittipaldi & D.Hulme. 1975: E.Fittipaldi & E.Mass. 1976: J.Hunt & E.Mass. 1977: J.Hunt & E.Mass. 1978: J.Hunt & P.Tambay. 1979: J.Watson & P.Tambay. 1980: J.Watson & A.Prost. 1981: J.Watson & A.de Cesaris. 1982: N.Lauda & J.Watson. 1983: N.Lauda & J.Watson. 1984: N.Lauda & A.Prost. 1985: N.Lauda, A.Prost & J.Watson. 1986: A.Prost & K.Rosberg. 1987: A.Prost & S.Johansson. 1988:

A.Prost & A.Senna. 1989: A.Prost & A.Senna. 1990: A.Senna & G.Berger.
1991: A.Senna & G.Berger. 1992: A.Senna & G.Berger. 1993: A.Senna,
M.Andretti & M.Hakkinen. 1994: M.Hakkinen, M.Brundle & P.Alliot. 1995:
N.Mansell, M.Blundell* & M.Hakkinen. *For first two Grand Prix only.*

Minardi

Minardi Team Spa
Via Spalenzani 21, 48018 Faunze (Ra), Italy
Tel: +39 546 620480   Fax: +39 546 620998

Brief History

1979: Minardi formed by Gain Carlo Minardi. 1985: Minardi make their
Formula One debut in Brazil. 1988: Pierluigi Martini picks up Minardi's first
points with sixth in Canada. 1990: Minardi record their only front row start
with Martini behind Gerhard Berger in America. 1993: Christian Fittipaldi
takes Minardi's highest placing of fourth in South Africa. Minardi's best
finish of eighth with seven points in the Constructors' World Championship.

Grand Prix Results

Contested:	155
Victories:	0
Pole Positions:	0
Fastest Laps:	0
Constructors' World Titles:	0 (Best: 7th 1991)
Drivers' World Championships:	0 (Best: 10th 1994)
Most Points in a Season:	7 (1993)
Total World Championship Points:	26

Review – Seven race itch

It was a season of two halves for Minardi. They took five points with three
top six finishes to end tenth in the Constructors' World Championship.
However, those points all came from the first seven races with Alboreto sixth
in Monaco, and Martini taking fifth at Barcelona and Magny Cours.

Their main problem was getting to the end of races with more than half the
starts of Martini and Michele Alboreto ending prematurely. Martini will look
to improve on his nine finishes as he enters his eighth season driving with the
team and will be partnered by Luca Badoer for the 1995 season which looks
set to be another difficult one for the Italian team.

Drivers and Results 1994

Driver	Country	Races	Pts	Psn	Com	Ret	F
Pierluigi Martini	Italy	16	4	=18th	9	7	0
Michele Alboreto	Italy	16	1	=24th	6	10	0

Grand Prix	Pierluigi Martini	Michele Alboreto
Brazil	8th	Retired
Pacific	Retired	Retired
San Marino	Retired	Retired
Monaco	Retired	6th
Spain	5th	Retired
Canada	9th	11th
France	5th	Retired
Great Britain	10th	Retired
Germany	Retired	Retired
Hungary	Retired	7th
Belgium	8th	9th
Italy	Retired	Retired
Portugal	12th	13th
Europe	15th	14th
Japan	Retired	Retired
Australia	9th	Retired

Car Specifications 1995

Sponsors:	Agip, Magneti Marelli, Xtrac, Penske & Brembo
Chairman:	Gain Carlo Minardi
Designer:	Aldo Costa
Team Manager:	Renato Cappucci
Chief Mechanic:	Gabriele Pagliarini
Drivers:	Pierluigi Martini & Luca Badoer
Test Driver:	Gian Carlo Fisichella

Engine:	**Ford**
Type:	EDM
Cylinders:	8
Injection:	Magneti Marelli
Electronics:	Magneti Marelli
Fuel:	Agip
Oil:	Agip

Transmission:	**Minardi**
Gearbox:	6 speed plus reverse
Gear Selection:	Xtrac

Dimensions

Overall Length:	4350mm	Wheelbase:	2840mm
Front Track:	1687mm	Rear Track:	1621mm
Overall Width:	1980mm	Height:	995mm

Chassis

Front/Rear Suspension: Inboard spring via rocker and pushrod to wishbone

Dampers:	Penske	Tyres:	Goodyear
Brake Pads:	Carbon Industrie	Brake Discs:	Brembo
Brake Calipers:	Brembo		

Wheel Diameter (Front/Rear): 11" & 13"
Wheel Rim Widths (Front/Rear): 13.7" & 13"

Engines 1985-95

1985-87 – Motori Moderni Turbo. 1988-90 – Ford Cosworth. 1991 – Ferrari. 1992 – Lamborghini. 1993-95 – Ford Cosworth.

Drivers 1985-95

1985: P.Martini. 1986: A.de Cesaris & A.Nannini. 1987: A.Nannini & A.Campos. 1988: L.Perez Sala, A.Campos & P.Martini. 1989: P.Martini, L.Perez Sala & P.Barilla. 1990: P.Martini, P.Barilla & G.Morbidelli. 1991: P.Martini, G.Morbidelli & R.Moreno. 1992: G.Morbidelli, C.Fittipaldi & A.Zanardi. 1993: C.Fittipaldi, F.Barbazza, P.Martini & J-M.Gounon. 1994: P.Martini & M.Alboreto. 1995: P.Martini & L.Badoer.

Pacific Lotus

Pacific Team Lotus
Brunel Business Centre, Brunel Way, Thetford, Norfolk, IP24 1HP
Tel: +44 (0)1842 755724   Fax: +44 (0)1842 755714

Pacific Brief History

1994: Pacific enter Formula One but fail to finish a race all season. 1995:
Merge with Lotus to form Pacific Team Lotus for second season in F1.

Grand Prix Record

Team	Pacific	Lotus
Contested:	5	490
Victories:	0	79
Pole Positions:	0	107
Fastest Laps:	0	71
Constructors' World Titles:	0	7
Most Points in a Season:	0	92 (1973)
Total World Championship Points:	0	1317 (1352)

Review – A drop in the ocean

Pacific found that the jump into Formula One is not an easy one. Having
survived their debut season, and with financial input from Japan and the
'merger' with Lotus for 1995, they will go into the new season thinking that
things can only get better. They qualified for five of the opening six races of
last season, and this was due more to the misfortunes of others rather than
their own car or drivers.

Jean-Paul Belmondo qualified for only two races in Monaco and Spain, while
Bertrand Gachot only failed to qualify in Aida out of the first six races. From
Canada in June onwards, the Pacific team leaving for home on Saturday
evening became a familiar sight to Grand Prix watchers. 1995 should not be
quite as bad as last year. If nothing else they should have learnt a great deal
from sniffing around the other teams in the little time they spent in the pit
lane on race day. They have a bit more money to work with this year, and the
deal with Lotus can only be of benefit to them especially in terms of making
them more attractive to potential sponsors.

For Lotus, one of the proudest names in Formula One, the 1990s saw the
gradual decline of the previous years, gathering speed with Peter Collins and

Peter Wright taking over the team in 1991. The last season saw Lotus finish pointless for the first time in 39 Constructors' World Championships. The team had acquired the Mugen-Honda engine, and a discontented Johnny Herbert left for Ligier and then Benetton after thirteen of the sixteen race season with odd drivers filling in for the final three races of the season. The team were placed in the hands of receivers with debts approaching £10 million pounds and after a temporary lay-off at the end of the year, Lotus couldn't continue although the name has been given a new lease of life with their Pacific merger.

Pacific Drivers and Results 1994

Driver	Country	Races	Pts	Psn	Com	Ret	F
Bertrand Gachot	Belgium	5	–	–	0	5	11
Paul Belmondo	France	2	–	–	0	2	14

Grand Prix	Bertrand Gachot	Paul Belmondo
Brazil	Retired	FQ
Pacific	FQ	FQ
San Marino	Retired	FQ
Monaco	Retired	Retired
Spain	Retired	Retired
Canada	Retired	FQ
France	FQ	FQ
Great Britain	FQ	FQ
Germany	FQ	FQ
Hungary	FQ	FQ
Belgium	FQ	FQ
Italy	FQ	FQ
Portugal	FQ	FQ
Europe	FQ	FQ
Japan	FQ	FQ
Australia	FQ	FQ

Lotus Drivers and Results 1994

Driver	Country	Races	Pts	Psn	Com	Ret	F
Johnny Herbert*	Great Britain	16	–	–	8	5	0
Pedro Lamy	Portugal	4	–	–	3	1	0
Alessandro Zanardi	Italy	10	–	–	4	6	0
Philippe Adams	Belgium	2	–	–	1	1	0
Eric Bernard†	France	14	–	–	1	0	0
Mika Salo	Finland	2	–	–	1	1	0

Herbert also had one race for Ligier and two races for Benetton.
†*Bernard also had 13 races for Ligier.*

Grand Prix	Herbert	Lamy	Zanardi	Adams	Bernard	Salo
Brazil	7th	10th	–	–	–	–
Pacific	7th	8th	–	–	–	–
San Marino	10th	Retired	–	–	–	–
Monaco	Retired	11th	–	–	–	–
Spain	Retired	–	9th	–	–	–
Canada	8th	–	Retired	–	–	–
France	7th	–	Retired	–	–	–
Great Britain	11th	–	Retired	–	–	–
Germany	Retired	–	Retired	–	–	–
Hungary	Retired	–	13th	–	–	–
Belgium	12th	–	–	Retired	–	–
Italy	Retired	–	Retired	–	–	–
Portugal	11th	–	–	16th	–	–
Europe	–	–	16th	–	18th	–
Japan	–	–	13th	–	–	10th
Australia	–	–	Retired	–	–	Retired

Car Specifications 1995

Sponsors: Ursus, Catamaran, Hewlett-Packard, Igol, Quest International, Bellerose, Interflora, Kenwood, Mira, Cargo Express, Sally Ferries, Malcom Andrews, Chell Instruments.
Owner: Keith Wiggins
Designer: Frank Coppuck (Chief), Peter Elleray
Team Manager: Ian Dawson
Chief Mechanic: Jerry Bond
Drivers: Bertrand Gachot, Andrea Montermini & JJ Lehto

Engine: **Ford**
Type: Cosworth ED
Cylinders: V8
Maximum RPM: 13,500
Electronics: Cosworth Electronics
Fuel: ATL Fuel cell
Oil: Pacific designed system

Transmission: **Pacific**
Gearbox: Six Speed semi-authomatic longitudinal
Clutch: AP

Chassis
Front Suspension: Pushrod   Rear Suspension: Pushrod
Dampers: Penske
Brake Pads: Carbone Industrie   Brake Discs: Carbone Industrie
Brake Calipers: AP 6-pot at front; AP 4-pot at rear

Steering:	Pacific	Radiators:	Secan
Wheels:	Dymag		

Pacific Engine 1994

Ilmor – 1994

Lotus Engines 1958-94

1958-65 – Climax. 1966 – BRM. 1967-83 – Ford. 1984-86 – Renault Turbo. 1987-88 – Honda. 1989 – Judd. 1990 – Lamborghini. 1991 – Judd. 1992-93 – Ford. 1994 – Mugen-Honda.

Pacific Drivers 1994

1994 – J-P.Belmondo & B.Gachot

Lotus Drivers 1958-95

1958: C.Allison & G.Hill. 1959: I.Ireland & G.Hill. 1960: S.Moss, I.Ireland, J.Surtees, J.Clark & D.Piper. 1961: S.Moss, I.Ireland, J.Clark & T.Taylor. 1962: J.Clark, T.Taylor & P.Arundell. 1963: J.Clark & T.Taylor. 1964: J.Clark, P.Arundell & M.Spence. 1965: J.Clark & M.Spence. 1966: J.Clark, M.Spence & P.Arundell. 1967: J.Clark & G.Hill. 1968: J.Clark, G.Hill & J.Oliver. 1969: G.Hill, J.Rindt, M.Andretti, J.Miles & R.Attwood. 1970: J.Rindt, R.Wisell, E.Fittipaldi & J.Miles. 1971: E.Fittipaldi & R.Wisell. 1972: E.Fittipaldi & R.Wisell. 1973: E.Fittipaldi & R.Peterson. 1974: R.Peterson & J.Ickx. 1975: R.Peterson, J.Ickx, J.Watson & J.Crawford. 1976: M.Andretti, R.Peterson & G.Nilsson. 1977: M.Andretti & G.Nilsson. 1978: M.Andretti, R.Peterson & J-P Jarier. 1979: M.Andretti & C.Reutemann. 1980: M.Andretti, E.de Angelis & N.Mansell. 1981: E.de Angelis & N.Mansell. 1982: E.de Angelis, N.Mansell & G.Lees. 1983: E.de Angelis & N.Mansell. 1984: E.de Angelis & N.Mansell. 1985: E.de Angelis & A.Senna. 1986: J.Dumfries & A.Senna. 1987: S.Nakajima & A.Senna. 1988: N.Piquet & S.Nakajima. 1989: N.Piquet & S.Nakajima. 1990: D.Warwick, M.Donnelly & J.Herbert. 1991: M.Hakkinen, J.Bailey & J.Herbert. 1992: M.Hakkinen & J.Herbert. 1993: J.Herbert, A.Zanardi & P.Lamy. 1994: J.Herbert, A.Zanardi, P.Lamy, E.Bernard, M.Salo & P.Adams. 1995: B.Gachot, A.Montermini & JJ Lehto.

Sauber

PP Sauber AG
Wildbachstrasse 9, 8340 Hinwil, Switzerland
Tel: +41 193 81400   Fax: +41 193 81670

Brief History

1993: Sauber record a scoring finish in their first Grand Prix with JJ Lehto taking fifth in South Africa. The team end the season sixth in the Constructors' World Championship with 12 points.

Grand Prix Record

Contested:	32
Victories:	0
Pole Positions:	0
Fastest Laps:	0
Constructors' World Championships:	0 (Best: 6th 1993)
Drivers' World Championships:	0 (Best: 8th 1994)
Most Points in a Season:	12 (1993 & 1994)
Total World Championship Points:	24

Review – Exciting times ahead?

The 1994 campaign was a mixed one for the Swiss team who possess a potentially exciting driver line-up that could bring rewards in the 1995 season.

Karl Wendlinger started the season well with sixth in the first race in Brazil followed two races later with fourth in San Marino, but his season was to be halted in Monte Carlo. Wendlinger crashed his Sauber into the barriers and was left in a coma for three weeks fighting for his life. The pictures of him being attended at the trackside have left a lasting impression on all that saw them and feared the worst. At a difficult time for the whole team, Heinz-Harald Frentzen continued Wendlinger's good work and built on his own fifth place in Aida with fourth in France and sixth in Jerez and Suzuka. Andrea de Cesaris picked up the team's only other point with sixth at Magny Cours after he replaced the injured Wendlinger.

Wendlinger returns to partner Frentzen for 1995 having nearly surprised the sport at the end of the season by talking about competing in the last few races of last year. The team have continued to improve since the Austrian's crash in Monaco, and few people will begrudge Sauber the success that their hard work and enthusiasm have brought them. Wendlinger and Frentzen are an exciting driver package and the initiative that they have grasped in their first 32 Grand Prix can be built upon for certain success in the very near future.

Drivers and Results 1994

Driver	Country	Races	Pts	Psn	Com	Ret	F
Heinz-Harald Frentzen	Germany	16	7	13th	7	8	1
Karl Wendlinger	Austria	4	4	=18th	2	1	1
Andrea de Cesaris*	Italy	9	4	=18th	1	8	0
JJ Lehto†	Finland	2	1	=25th	1	1	0

de Cesaris also had two races and scored three points for Jordan.
† Lehto also had six races and scored one point for Benetton.

Grand Prix	Frentzen	Wendlinger	de Cesaris	JJ Lehto
Brazil	Retired	6th	–	–
Pacfic	5th	Retired	–	–
San Marino	7th	4th	–	–
Monaco	FS	FS	–	–
Spain	Retired	–	–	–
Canada	Retired	–	Retired	–
France	4th	–	6th	–
Great Britain	7th	–	Retired	–
Germany	Retired	–	Retired	–
Hungary	Retired	–	Retired	–
Belgium	Retired	–	Retired	–
Italy	Retired	–	Retired	–
Portugal	Retired	–	Retired	–
Europe	6th	–	Retired	–
Japan	6th	–	–	Retired
Australia	7th	–	–	10th

Car Specifications 1995

Sponsors:	Red Bull
Owner:	Peter Sauber
Designer:	Leo Ress
Team Manager:	Beat Zehnder
Chief Mechanic:	Daniel Christ
Drivers:	Karl Wendlinger and Heinz-Harald Frentzen
Test Driver:	Norberto Fontana
Engine:	**Ford**
Type:	Zetec-R

Cylinders:	8
Injection:	Cosworth
Spark Plugs:	Champion
Electronics:	Ford
Fuel:	Elf, ATL tanks
Oil:	Elf
Instruments:	Ford, PI Research

Transmission: **Sauber**

Gearbox:	Longitudinal, 6-speed
Gear Selection:	Semi-automatic
Drive Shafts:	MAT
Clutch:	Sachs

Dimensions

Overall Length:	4340mm	Wheelbase:	2900mm
Front Track:	1710mm	Rear Track:	1610mm
Overall Width:	2000mm	Height:	950mm

Chassis

Front Suspension:	Pushrod	Rear Suspension:	Pushrod
Dampers:	Sachs	Tyres:	Goodyear
Brake Pads:	Carbone	Brake Discs:	Carbone
Brake Calipers:	Brembo	Radiators:	Behr
Steering:	Sauber		

Wheel Diameter (Front/Rear): 13.9" & 11"
Wheel Rim Widths (Front/Rear): 12" & 13"

Engines 1993-95

1993 – Sauber. 1994 – Mercedes. 1995 – Ford.

Drivers 1993-95

1993: K.Wendlinger & J.J.Lehto. 1994: K.Wendlinger, H-H.Frentzen,
J.J.Lehto & A.de Cesaris. 1995: H-H.Frentzen & K.Wendlinger.

Simtek

Simtek Grand Prix
8 Wates Way, Acre Estate, Wildmere Road, Banbury, Oxon, OX16 7TS
Tel: +44 (0)1295 265998   Fax: +44 (0)1295 265975

Brief History

1989: Simtek Research founded by Nick Wirth and Max Mosley. 1993:
Grand Prix project formed in the spring, with confirmation of entry to 1994
World Championship announced at the end of the year.

Grand Prix Record

Contested:	16
Victories:	0
Pole Positions:	0
Fastest Laps:	0
Constructors' World Championships:	0
Drivers' World Championships:	0
Most Points in a Season:	0
Total World Championship Points:	0

Review – Debut depression

It is doubtful if a team entering its first year in F1 could have suffered so
much trauma as Simtek. Certainly 1994 proved to be a season that would
have tested even one of the established teams to its limits. That Simtek
continue for 1995 says much about their spirit and will to succeed.

David Brabham, son of three times World Champion Jack, was announced as
the Simtek team leader shortly before they confirmed they would enter the
1994 FIA Formula One World Championship using a Ford Cosworth engine.

Two weeks before the start of the season, Roland Ratzenberger was
announced as second driver to Brabham who completes the Brazilian Grand
Prix in 12th position. Ratzenberger finished 11th at the Pacific Grand Prix but
just two weeks later in San Marino his Simtek seemed to go out of control in
a qualifying session and flew into a concrete wall giving him little chance of
survival. In Spain, the team suffered another blow when new driver Andrea
Montermini crashed badly but thankfully sustained only slight injuries from
an accident that could have been far worse had the car not stood up so well to
the impact.

114

At the British Grand Prix at Silverstone in July Simtek at last had cause for celebration when both cars finished a race for the first time, David Brabham leading team-mate Jean-Marc Gounon in 16th place. Brabham though, received a one race ban suspended for three races when he went off and took a piece of Jean Alesi with him in Portugal. In Jerez Mimmo Schiattarella finished his debut in 19th place, with Takachiho Inoue driving in Japan having raised sufficient funds for a race. The team's best finish in their first season was Jean-Marc Gounon's ninth in France, while David Brabham's best was 10th in Spain.

After the hell Simtek went through in the first half of the season with Ratzenberger's death and the accident involving Montermini, they came through to complete their campaign to earn great respect. Their major sponsors have all signed up for the new season, and 1995 should produce some slow but steady progress. They can approach 1995 knowing that it will be better than 1994.

Drivers and Results 1994

Driver	Country	Races	Pts	Psn	Com	Ret	F
David Brabham	Australia	16	–	–	6	10	0
Roland Ratzenberger	Austria	1	–	–	1	0	1
Andrea Montermini	Italy	0	–	–	0	0	0
Jean-Marc Gounon	France	7	–	–	4	3	0
Mimmo Schattarella	Italy	2	–	–	1	1	0
Taki Inoue	Japan	1	–	–	0	1	0

Grand Prix	Brabham	Ratz'ger	Gounon	Schiat'lla	Inoue
Brazil	12th	FQ	–	–	–
Pacific	Retired	11th	–	–	–
San Marino	Retired	FS	–	–	–
Monaco	Retired	–	–	–	–
Spain*	10th	–	–	–	–
Canada	14th	–	–	–	–
France	Retired	–	9th	–	–
Great Britain	15th	–	16th	–	–
Germany	Retired	–	Retired	–	–
Hungary	11th	–	Retired	–	–
Belgium	Retired	–	11th	–	–
Italy	Retired	–	Retired	–	–
Portugal	Retired	–	15th	–	–
Europe	Retired	–	–	19th	–
Japan	12th	–	–	–	Ret.
Australia	Retired	–	–	Retired	–

* Andrea Montermini crashed during practice in Spain and failed to start a Grand Prix in 1994.

Car Specifications 1995

Sponsors:	Champion, Xtrac, Penske, Secan, Brembo, SEP & Hitco
Owner:	Nick Wirth
Designer:	Nick Wirth
Team Manager:	Charlie Moody
Chief Mechanic:	Dave Luckett
Drivers:	Jos Verstappen and Mimmo Schiatterella/Hideki Noda (Shared)

Engine:	**Ford**
Type:	EDB
Cylinders:	8
Injection:	Cosworth Engineering
Spark Plugs:	Champion

Transmission:	**Xtrac**
Gearbox:	6SP Longitudinal
Clutch:	AP

Dimensions

Overall Length:	4000mm	Wheelbase:	2800 mm
Front Track:	1700mm	Rear Track:	1600mm
Overall Width:	2000mm	Height:	1000mm

Chassis

Front Suspension:	Pushrod	Rear Suspension:	Pushrod
Dampers:	Penske	Tyres:	Goodyear
Brake Pads:	SEP/Hitco	Brake Discs:	SEP/Hitco
Brake Calipers:	Brembo		
Radiators:	Secan		
Wheels:	Dymag		
Dry Weight:	595kg (including driver in complete racing apparel)		

Engine 1994-95

1994-95 – Ford.

Drivers 1994-95

1994: D.Brabham, R.Ratzenberger, A.Montermini, J-M.Gounon, M.Schiattarella & T.Inoue. 1995: J.Verstappen, H.Noda & M.Sciattarella.

Tyrrell

Tyrrell Racing Organisation Ltd
Long Reach, Ockham, Woking, Surrey, GU23 6PE
Tel: +44 (0)1483 284955   Fax: +44 (0)1483 284892

Brief History

1970: Jackie Stewart takes pole position for Tyrrell in Montreal in their first race in Formula One. 1971: Stewart wins the second race of the season in Spain to record Tyrrell's first win in only their fifth race and go onto win the Constructors' World Championship with more than double the points of second placed BRM. 1972: Tyrrell win four races but finish second to Lotus in the Championship. 1973: Five races won but runners-up to Lotus for the second year running. 1978: Patrick Depailler wins in Monaco for his only Grand Prix win for Tyrrell. 1982: Michele Alboreto wins in Las Vegas for Tyrrell's first win for four years. 1983: Alboreto wins in Detroit for Tyrrell's last victory to date. 1984: Tyrrell fail to score a point in the Constructors' Championship for the first time. 1989: After six years without success, Jonathan Palmer records the fastest lap in the Canadian Grand Prix.

Grand Prix Record

Contested:	352
Victories:	23
Pole Positions:	14
Fastest Laps:	20
Constructors' World Championships:	1
Drivers' World Championships:	2
Most Points in a Season:	82 (1973)
Total World Championship Points:	592

Review – Percentage game the key

Tyrrell recovered from failing to achieve a top six finish in 1993 to pick up 13 points and finish equal sixth place in the Constructors' World Championship last season with their Yamaha engines. Britain's Mark Blundell picked up a podium finish with third in Spain having finished just one of his previous four Grand Prix but then recorded consecutive fifth placings in Hungary and Belgium in the second half of the season. He was partnered in 1994 by Japan's Ukyo Katayama who was consistently good when he could finish a race. He completed only four of sixteen but was fifth twice, sixth and seventh in those where he actually reached the chequered flag.

For 1995 Tyrrell feel that the regulation changes could suit them and should see a similar year to that of 1994. Tyrrell should score points and could improve their tally from this season if Katayama can reach the end of a few more races. Although seven of last year's retirements were due to the car, a record of only finishing 25% of races is not good.

Drivers and Results 1994

Driver	Country	Races	Pts	Psn	Com	Ret	F
Ukyo Katayama	Japan	16	5	17th	4	12	0
Mark Blundell	Great Britain	16	8	12th	7	9	0

Grand Prix	Ukyo Katajama	Mark Blundell
Brazil	5th	Retired
Pacific	Retired	Retired
San Marino	5th	9th
Monaco	Retired	Retired
Spain	Retired	3rd
Canada	Retired	10th
France	Retired	10th
Great Britain	6th	Retired
Germany	Retired	Retired
Hungary	Retired	5th
Belgium	Retired	5th
Italy	Retired	Retired
Portugal	Retired	Retired
Europe	7th	13th
Japan	Retired	Retired
Australia	Retired	Retired

Car Specifications 1995

Sponsors:	Nokia, Fondmetal, Mild Seven, Club Angle, Hoxsin Futures, Calbee, APN777 Zent, Simpson, Fiamm & Motion
Chairman:	Ken Tyrrell
Designer:	Dr. Harvey Postlethwaite
Team Manager:	Rupert Mainwaring
Chief Mechanic:	Chris White
Drivers:	Ukyo Katayama & Mika Salo
Engine:	**Yamaha**
Type:	OX10C
Cylinders:	10

Injection:	Zytek
Spark Plugs:	NGK
Fuel:	Sasol
Oil:	Sasol

Transmission: **Tyrrell**

Gearbox:	Tyrrell 6 Speed
Gear Selection:	Pneumatic, sequential
Drive Shafts:	Tyrrell
Clutch:	AP

Dimensions

Overall Length:	4380mm	Wheelbase:	2890mm
Front Track:	1700mm	Rear Track:	1610mm
Overall Width:	2000mm	Height:	950mm

Chassis

Front Suspension:	Tyrrell	Rear Suspension:	Tyrrell
Dampers:	Koni	Tyres:	Goodyear
Brake Pads:	Hitco Carbon	Brake Discs:	Hitco Carbon
Steering:	Tyrrell	Fuel Tanks:	ATL
Instruments:	PI Reseach System V		

Wheel Diameter (Front/Rear): 11" & 13"

Wheel Rim Widths (Front/Rear): 11" & 13"

Engines 1970-95

1970-85 – Ford. 1985-86 – Renault Turbo. 1987-90 – Ford. 1991 - Honda. 1992 – Ilmor. 1993-95 – Yamaha.

Drivers 1970-95

1970: J.Stewart & F.Cevert. 1971: J.Stewart & F.Cevert. 1972: J.Stewart & F.Cevert. 1973: J.Stewart & F.Cevert. 1974: J.Scheckter & P.Depailler. 1975: J.Scheckter & P.Depailler. 1976: J.Scheckter & P.Depailler. 1977: R.Peterson & P.Depailler. 1978: P.Depailler & D.Pironi. 1979: J-P.Jarier & D.Pironi. 1980: J-P.Jarrier, D.Daly & M.Thackwell. 1981: E.Cheever, R.Zunino & M.Alboreto. 1982: M.Alboreto, B.Henton & S.Borgudd. 1983: M.Alboreto & D.Sullivan. 1984: S.Bellof, M.Brundle, S.Johansson & M.Thackwell. 1985: M.Brundle, S.Johansson, S.Bellof, I.Capelli & P.Streiff. 1986: M.Brundle & P.Streiff. 1987: J.Palmer & P.Streiff. 1988: J.Palmer & J.Bailey. 1989: J.Palmer, M.Alboreto, J.Alesi & J.Herbert. 1990: S.Nakajima & J.Alesi. 1991: S.Nakajima & S.Modena. 1992: A.de Cesaris & O.Grouillard. 1993: A.de Cesaris & U.Katayama. 1994: U.Katayama & M.Blundell. 1995: U.Katayama & M.Salo

Williams

Williams Grand Prix Engineering Ltd
Basil Hill Road, Didcot, Oxfordshire, OX11 7HW
Tel: +44 (0)1235 815161   Fax: +44 (0)1235 816660

Brief History

1969: After building his business up, Frank Williams starts running cars.
1970: Piers Courage killed during the Dutch Grand Prix driving a private
session. 1973: Entered Formula One under the name of ISO. 1976:
Disappointing partnership with oil man Walter Wolf. 1978: Williams Grand
Prix Engineering founded. Australian Alan Jones signed to drive. 1979: Clay
Regazzoni wins in Britain for Williams' first Grand Prix victory. 1980: Alan
Jones wins the Drivers' World Championship with Williams taking the
Constructors' title for the first time. 1986: Frank Williams seriously injured in
a car crash and confined to a wheelchair. 1992: Nigel Mansell becomes the
first driver to win the opening five rounds of a season and achieves a record
of nine victories in total as Williams' take the Drivers' and Constructors'
World Championships. 1993: Alan Prost wins his fourth World title and
announces his retirement from the sport. 1994: Williams record their seventh
Constructors' Championship victory to bring them level with Lotus in the all-
time record.

Grand Prix Record

Contested:	329
Victories:	78
Pole Positions:	73
Fastest Laps:	81
Constructors' World Championships:	7
Drivers' World Championships:	5
Most Points in a Season:	168
Total World Championship Points:	1512.5

Review – Death, joy, disappointment

To say 1994 was one of the most hectic and numbing years in the history of
the Williams race team would be a gross understatement. After finally
persuading triple World Champion Ayrton Senna to sit in one of his cars,
Frank Williams saw the Brazilian killed whilst competing in the San Marino
Grand Prix in Imola. The loss to the sport and to the Williams team was

immense, but the season continued with Damon Hill moving up to the position of team leader and young Scotsman David Coulthard turning from test driver to Grand Prix star.

Hill had taken second to Michael Schumacher in the opening race in Brazil, and after Schumacher had almost equalled Mansell's feat of five straight wins from the start of the season, he started to eat into the German's World Championship lead by taking victory in Spain and second in Canada and France. He then won in front of his own fans at Silverstone – something his father Graham had never acheived – as Schumacher was disqualified for the infamous 'black flag' incident. After eighth in Germany, Hill put together a run of four wins and two seconds to take the Championship to the last race of the season in Australia before he and Schumacher collided in Adelaide, leaving Hill runner-up but Williams as Constructors' Champions.

David Coulthard drove in eight races following the death of Senna and it would have been twelve but for guest appearances by former World Champion Nigel Mansell in France, Europe, Japan and Australia for a reported £4 million fee. Coulthard showed extreme maturity as he was thrust into a situation that he would not even have had time to dream about. After two fifth places and three retirements in his first five races, he finished with fourth, sixth and second in Belgium, Italy and Portugal respectively.

Mansell retired at Magny Cours and Jerez, but picked up fourth at Suzuka after a lengthy scrap with Jean Alesi. He went on to win in Adelaide with all the attention focused on the coming together of his team-mate and Schumacher.

Having taken their third consecutive Constructors' World Championship last season there is every chance that Williams will match the feat of four-straight wins achieved by McLaren between 1988-91. Having said that, they would not have completed the hat-trick had Benetton had a regular points scorer in their second car last year.

After all the discussions about whether Coulthard or Mansell should support Hill in 1995, Williams will just be pleased to start the new season and put the emotions of San Marino in May of 1994 behind them. They have a proven car and by the end of the season they could also have a proven driver combination. Although he was by far the cheaper option, Coulthard represents the future, and having been given his chance in 1994 he deserved to show what he can do over a full season of testing, qualifying and competing and we await his first full season with anticipation.

Drivers and Results 1994

Driver	Country	Races	Pts	Psn	Com	Ret	F
Ayrton Senna	Brazil	3	–		0	3	0
Damon Hill	Great Britain	16	91	2nd	13	3	0
David Coulthard	Great Britain	8	14	8th	4	4	0
Nigel Mansell	Great Britain	4	13	9th	2	2	0

Grand Prix	Senna	Hill	Coulthard	Mansell
Brazil	Retired	2nd	–	–
Pacific	Retired	Retired	–	–
San Marino	Retired	6th	–	–
Monaco	–	Retired	–	–
Spain	–	1st	Retired	–
Canada	–	2nd	5th	–
France	–	2nd	–	Retired
Great Britain	–	1st	Retired	–
Germany	–	8th	Retired	–
Hungary	–	2nd	Retired	–
Belgium	–	1st	4th	–
Italy	–	1st	6th	–
Portugal	–	1st	2nd	–
Europe	–	2nd	–	Retired
Japan	–	1st	–	4th
Australia	–	Retired	–	1st

Car Specifications 1995

Sponsors:	Rothmans, Elf, Goodyear, Sparco, Magneti Marelli, Sanyo, Andersen Consulting & Labatt
Owner:	Frank Williams
Designer:	Adrian Newey
Team Manager:	Dickie Stanford
Chief Mechanic:	Carl Gaden
Drivers:	Damon Hill & David Coulthard
Test Driver:	Jean-Christophe Boullion

Engine:	**Renault V10**
Type:	RS7
Cylinders:	10
Spark Plugs:	Champion
Electronics:	Magneti Marelli
Fuel:	Elf
Oil:	Elf

Transmission:	**Williams**		
Gearbox:	6 Speed Semi-Automatic		
Clutch:	AP Racing		

Dimensions

Overall Length:	4150mm	Wheelbase:	2890mm
Front Track:	1670mm	Rear Track:	1600mm

Chassis

Front Suspension:	Williams	Rear Suspension:	Williams
Dampers:	Williams	Tyres:	Goodyear
Brake Pads:	Carbon Industrie	Brake Discs:	Carbon Industrie
Brake Calipers:	AP Racing	Instruments:	Magneti Marelli

Wheel Diameter (Front/Rear): 13" & 11"
Wheel Rim Widths (Front/Rear): 13" & 13.7"

Engines 1973-95

1973-83 – Ford. 1984-87 – Honda Turbo. 1988 – Judd. 1989-95 – Renault.

Drivers 1973-95

1973: H.Ganley, H.Pescarolo, & N.Galli. 1974: A.Merzario, J-P.Jabouille & T.Belso. 1975: A.Merzario, J.Laffite & J.Scheckter. 1976: J.Ickx, M.Leclerc & A.Merzario. 1977: P.Neve. 1978: A.Jones. 1979: A.Jones & C.Regazzoni. 1980: A.Jones & C.Reutemann. 1981: A.Jones & C.Reutemann. 1982: K.Rosberg, D.Daly, C.Reuteman & M.Andretti. 1983: K.Rosberg, J.Laffite & J.Palmer. 1984: K.Rosberg & J.Laffite. 1985: K.Rosberg & N.Mansell. 1986: N.Mansell & N.Piquet. 1987: N.Mansell, N.Piquet & R.Patrese. 1988: N.Mansell, R.Patrese, M.Brundle & J.Schlesser. 1989: T.Boutsen & R.Patrese. 1990: T.Boutsen & R.Patrese. 1991: N.Mansell & R.Patrese. 1992: N.Mansell & R.Patrese. 1993: A.Prost & D.Hill. 1994: A.Senna, D.Hill, D.Couthard & N.Mansell. 1995: D.Hill & D.Coulthard.

Ayrton Senna 1960-1994 seen here in a McLaren

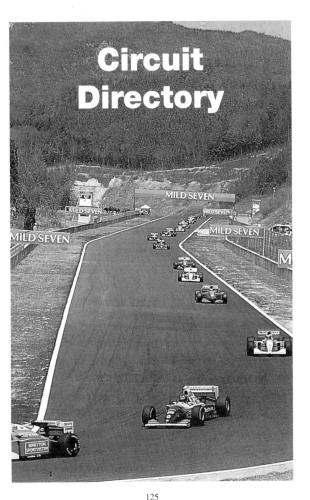

Circuit
Directory

Adelaide

Lap Distance: 2.349 miles / 3.780 km
Race Distance: 190.155 miles / 306.180 km – 81 laps

1. Turn One

From the startline, this fast left-right-left chicane is approached on a flying lap in fifth before being taken in fourth.

2. Wakefield Road

The cars enter close to the wall before straightening up and accelerating into fifth.

3. Wakefield Corner

This is guarded by a series of bumps on the approach making this sharp right hander a very uncomfortable proposition for the drivers, taken in second gear.

4. Flinders Street

This short straight is entered from a left hander that is equally as sharp as the previous right hander. Exited via another tight right hander in second gear.

5. East Terrace

After the slow entrance in second gear, the cars change quickly up to fourth before hitting a fast left flick followed immediately by a difficult right hander.

6. Rundle Road

Approached from a tight right hander in third, this is the second longest straight in the race.

7. Dequetteville Terrace

Otherwise known as Brabham Straight, this is the circuit's longest straight although overtaking opportunities are usually limited to the furthest end approaching the hairpin.

8. Roundabout

The slowest corner on the circuit. Taken in second gear, the approach contains several big bumps.

9. Racecourse

A fast but very bumpy right sweep that brings the cars back towards the finishing straight.

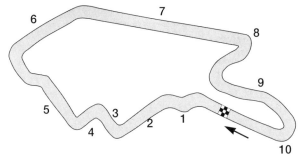

10. Fosters Corner

A right hand hairpin that slows the cars down into second gear guards the finishing straight.

Australia – 10 Year Record

Year	1st	2nd	3rd	4th	5th	6th
1985	Rosberg (Williams)	Laffite (Ligier)	Streiff (Ligier)	Capelli (Tyrrell)	Johansson (Ferrari)	Berger (Arrows)
1986	Prost (McLaren)	Piquet (Williams)	Johansson (Ferrari)	Brundle (Tyrrell)	Streiff (Tyrrell)	Dumfries (Lotus)
1987	Berger (Ferrari)	Alboreto (Ferrari)	Boutsen (Benetton)	Palmer (Tyrrell)	Dalmas (Lola)	Moreno (AGS)
1988	Prost (McLaren)	Senna (McLaren)	Piquet (Lotus)	Patrese (Williams)	Boutsen (Benetton)	Capelli (March)
1989	Boutsen (Williams)	Nannini (Benetton)	Patrese (Williams)	Nakajima (Louts)	Pirro (Benetton)	Martini (Minardi)
1990	Piquet (Benetton)	Mansell (Ferrari)	Prost (Ferrari)	Berger (McLaren)	Boutsen (Williams)	Patrese (Williams)
1991	Senna (McLaren)	Mansell (Williams)	Berger (McLaren)	Piquet (Benetton)	Patrese (Williams)	Morbidelli (Ferrari)
1992	Berger (Ferrari)	Schumacher (Benetton)	Brundle (Benetton)	Alesi (Ferrari)	Boutsen (Ligier)	Modena (Jordan)
1993	Senna (McLaren)	Prost (Williams)	Hill (Williams)	Alesi (Ferrari)	Berger (Ferrari)	Brundle (Ligier)
1994	Mansell (Williams)	Berger (Ferrari)	Brundle (McLaren)	Barrichello (Jordan)	Panis (Ligier)	Alesi (Ferrari)

Aida

Lap Distance   2.314 miles/3.723 km
Race Distance   192.06 miles/309.027 km – 83 laps

Used for the first time as a Grand Prix track in 1994 having previously been used domestically as a private track for anybody wealthy enough to pay a reputed £90,000 a head to join. Its inaugural race was a Sports Car race in 1990 and it has since hosted some Formula 3 and Touring Car races. It was widely reported that the billionaire owner, Hajima Tanaka, had paid almost £3m for the privilege of staging a Grand Prix at his private track. It is built in a wilderness and, with only one road serving it, the crowd was restricted to 70,000 from the 100,000 capacity.

Pacific – 10 Year Record

Year	1st	2nd	3rd	4th	5th	6th
1994	Schumacher	Berger	Barrichello	Fittipaldi	Frentzen	Comas
	(Benetton)	(Ferrari)	(Jordan)	(Arrows)	(Sauber)	(Larrousse)

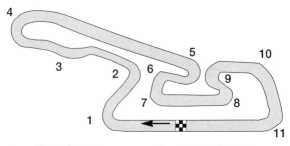

1.	**First Corner**	**7.**	**Piper Corner**
2.	**Williams Corner**	**8.**	**Redman Corner**
3.	**Moss S**	**9.**	**Hobbs Corner**
4.	**Attwood Curve**	**10.**	**Mike Knight Corner**
5.	**Hair Pin Corner**		
6.	**Revolver Corner**	**11.**	**Last Corner**

Buenos Aires

Lap Distance: 2.100 miles/3.380 km (Circuit No. 9)
                     2.585 miles/4.160 km (Circuit No. 6)

The 1995 season will see the first Grand Prix to be held in Argentina since 1981. It will be the 17th in all with the Autodromo Mudicipal de la Cuidad de Buenos Aires have played host to them all. It was the site of the first F1 race to incur fatalities when Farina's Ferrari killed nine spectators in the first race to be held there in 1953.

The track record is held by Nelson Piquet whose Barbham Ford BT49C recorded a time of 1m 45.287s on 12 April 1981. However, this was set on the larger Circuit 15 track. For the 1995 Grand Prix either the No 6 or No 9 circuit will be used.

The No 6 circuit utilises the whole outer loop of the illustration while the No 9 circuit includes the longer inner circuit.

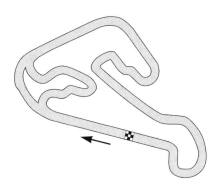

Catalunya

Lap Distance 2.949 miles/4.747 km
Race Distance 191.727 miles/308.855 km – 65 laps

1. Elf

The approach to Elf is downhill until almost the corner itself when it rises. This corner is taken in third on the inside so that the car can drift out to the left for the next bend before taking on the long right hander in fourth and fifth.

2. Repsol

This continues looping back on itself until the car hits the left hairpin at Seat (3) which has to be taken in second. Then it's time to accelerate up to fifth on a short straight.

4. Wurth

The car has to slow down to third for this sharp left hander.

5. Camposa

This right hander is blind but can be navigated safely in fourth leading to a fifth gear right-left chicane at Nissan.

6. Nissan

For this race the drivers, after the carnage of the previous few weeks, insisted a temporary tyre chicane was put up to slow the cars down on the run into the chicane.

7. La Caixa

Another short straight beckons before taking this left hander that keeps on sweeping left before changing direction into a long right hander.

8. Banc de Savadell

This is exited in fourth as the car accelerates towards the penultimate corner, another right hander that turns into a short straight leading to the final bend which is taken almost flat out in fifth. Then it's on to the home straight at about 150mph.

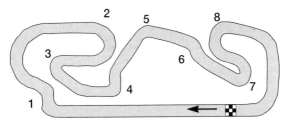

Spain – 10 Year Record

Year	1st	2nd	3rd	4th	5th	6th
Jerez						
1986	Senna (Lotus)	Mansell (Williams)	Prost (McLaren)	Rosberg (McLaren)	Fabi (Benetton)	Berger (Benetton)
1987	Mansell (Williams)	Prost (McLaren)	Johansson (McLaren)	Piquet (Williams)	Senna (Lotus)	Alliot (Lola)
1988	Prost (McLaren)	Mansell (Williams)	Nannini (Benetton)	Senna (McLaren)	Patrese (Williams)	Berger (Ferrari)
1989	Senna (McLaren)	Berger (Ferrari)	Prost (McLaren)	Alezi (Tyrrell)	Patrese (Williams)	Alliot (Lola)
1990	Prost (Ferrari)	Mansell (Ferrari)	Nannini (Benetton)	Boutsen (Williams)	Patrese (Williams)	Suzuki (Lola)
Catalunya						
1991	Mansell (Williams)	Prost (Ferrari)	Patrese (Williams)	Alesi (Ferrari)	Senna (McLaren)	Schumacher (Benetton)
1992	Mansell (Williams)	Schumacher (Benetton)	Alesi (Ferrari)	Berger (McLaren)	Alboreto (Footwork)	Martini (Dallara)
1993	Prost (Williams)	Senna (McLaren)	Schumacher (Benetton)	Patrese (Benetton)	Andretti (McLaren)	Berger (Ferrari)
1994	Hill (Williams)	Schumacher (Benetton)	Blundell (Tyrrell)	Alesi (Ferrari)	Martini (Minardi)	Irvine (Jordan)

Estoril

Lap Distance: 2.709 miles/4.350 km
Race Distance: 192.339 miles/308.848 km – 71 laps

---

1.   Pirelli Bridge
Approached at high speed this corner is entered in fifth and exited with the help of a low kerb.

3.   Martini Bridge
Almost immediately the cars enter into the second right hander which is taken flat out. Considered by most drivers to be more dangerous than the former Turn Eight, the barriers here are not far from the track and the corner tightens up very quickly.

4.   Turn Three
A very bumpy right hander taken in third with a late entry and apex causing bad understeer.

5.   Turn Five
More a kink than a corner it can be taken flat out but it does have a huge bump in the middle.

6.   Turn Six
Taken in third, this favours well balanced cars it has two appexes and tightens quickly.

7.   Turn Seven
An off-camber, downhill right hander that is negotiated in third.

8.   Turn Eight
Modified so that cars arrive at the corner much earlier than previously, it is a 120 degree turn followed by a straight of just 200 metres.

9.   Turn Nine
A new, very tight left hander taken in second. Many drivers have complained it is too slow.

10.   Turn Ten
The track climbs quite steeply to this long, open right hander bringing it back to the old track.

11.   Turn Eleven
A fast right hander that is taken in fourth as it is entered blind and tightens up quickly.

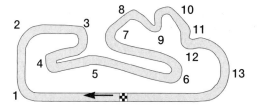

12. **Turn Twelve**

A very sharp left hander that is taken in second.

13. **Turn Thirteen**

A punishing right hand corner that seems to go on for ever before bringing the cars back on to the main straight. Re-named Senna in memory of the great Brazilian.

Portugal – 10 Year Record

Year	1st	2nd	3rd	4th	5th	6th
1985	Senna (Lotus)	Alboreto (Ferrari)	Tambay (Renault)	de Angelis (Lotus)	Mansell (Williams)	Bellof (Tyrell)
1986	Mansell (Williams)	Prost (McLaren)	Piquet (Williams)	Senna (Lotus)	Alboreto (Ferrari)	Johansson (Ferrari)
1987	Prost (McLaren)	Berger (Ferrari)	Piquet (Williams)	Fabi (Benetton)	Johansson (McLaren)	Cheever (Arrows)
1988	Prost (McLaren)	Capelli (March)	Boutsen (Benetton)	Warwick (Arrows)	Alboreto (Ferrari)	Senna (McLaren)
1989	Berger (Ferrari)	Prost (McLaren)	Johansson (Onyx)	Nannini (Benetton)	Martini (Minardi)	Palmer (Tyrell)
1990	Mansell (Ferrari)	Senna (McLaren)	Prost (Ferrari)	Berger (McLaren)	Piquet (Benetton)	Nannini (Benetton)
1991	Patrese Williams	Senna (McLaren)	Alesi (Ferrari)	Martini (Minardi)	Piquet (Benetton)	Schumacher (Benetton)
1992	Mansell (Williams)	Berger (McLaren)	Senna (McLaren)	Brundle (Benetton)	Hakkinen (Lotus)	Alboreto (Footwork)
1993	Schumacher (Benetton)	Prost (Williams)	Hill (Williams)	Alesi (Ferrari)	Wendlinger (Sauber)	Brundle (Ligier)
1994	Hill (Williams)	Coulthard (Williams)	Hakkinen (McLaren)	Barrichello (Jordan)	Verstappen (Benetton)	Brundle (McLaren)

Hockenheim

Lap Distance   4.235 miles/6.815 km
Race Distance   190.559 miles/306.675 km – 45 laps

1.   Turn One
A fast right hander that is taken in fourth and exited in fifth ready to move up to sixth and approximate 200mph for the long run to the first chicane.

2.   Bremskurve 1
Slowing to second gear for the right-left-right chicane. Prior to the race this chicane was re-named in memory of Jim Clark, the driver who died at the track.

3.   Bremskurve 2
The drivers are very busy on this particular stretch. The previous straight turns into a long right hand bend about 350 metres before...

4.   Ostkurve
The chicane which is a right-left taken in second gear leading into a long, fast right hander and on to the next straight.

5.   Bremskurve 3
Very bumpy and fast (fourth gear) at the approach and middle section, it is exited in fifth to get back into sixth for the next straight. Re-named after Ayrton Senna prior to the race.

6.   Agip kurve
A fast right hander that is taken at high speed, often still in fifth.

7.   Sachs kurve
Quickly down to second for the hairpin that has a well earned reputation for being slippy.

8.   Opel kurve
The final section in the stadium that leads back to the startline, the Opel kurve is a double apex hairpin taken in third and fourth before exiting on to the pits straight in

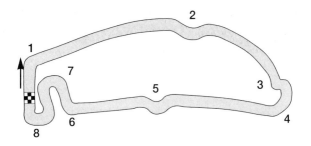

Germany – 10 Year Record

Year	1st	2nd	3rd	4th	5th	6th
Nurburgring						
1985	Alboreto (Ferrari)	Prost (McLaren)	Laffite (Renault)	Boutsen (Arrows)	Lauda (McLaren)	Mansell (Williams)
Hockenheim						
1986	Piquet (Williams)	Senna (Lotus)	Mansell (Williams)	Arnoux (Ligier)	Rosberg (McLaren)	Prost (McLaren)
1987	Piquet (Williams)	Johansson (McLaren)	Senna (Lotus)	Streiff (Tyrrell)	Palmer (Tyrrell)	Alliot (Lola)
1988	Senna (McLaren)	Prost (McLaren)	Berger (Ferrari)	Alboreto (Ferrari)	Capelli (March)	Boutsen (Benetton)
1989	Senna (McLaren)	Prost (McLaren)	Mansell (Ferrari)	Patrese (Williams)	Piquet (Lotus)	Warwick (Arrows)
1990	Senna (McLaren)	Nannini (Benetton)	Berger (McLaren)	Prost (Ferrari)	Patrese (Williams)	Boutsen (Williams)
1991	Mansell (Williams)	Patrese (Williams)	Alesi (Ferrari)	Berger (McLaren)	de Cesaris (Jordan)	Gachot (Jordan)
1992	Mansell (Williams)	Senna (McLaren)	Schumacher (Benetton)	Brundle (Benetton)	Alesi (Ferrari)	Comas (Ligier)
1993	Prost (Williams)	Schumacher (Benetton)	Brundell (Ligier)	Senna (McLaren)	Patrese (Benetton)	Berger (Ferrari)
1994	Berger (Ferrari)	Panis (Ligier)	Bernard (Ligier)	Fittipaldi (Arrows)	Morbidelli (Arrows)	Comas (Larrousse)

Hungaroring

Lap Distance   2.47 miles/3.975 km
Race Distance   189.851 miles/305.535 km – 77 laps

1.   Turn One
A long right-hand downhill bend entered in third, exited in fourth with just time to get up to fifth before slowing immediately to third for...

2.   Turn Two
There is a choice of two lines here but whether the car turns in early or late makes little difference to the amount of oversteer experienced as this long left hander begins to sweep right, which can be taken in fifth on to one of the few bumpy straights.

3.   Turn Three
Leaving the straight the driver cannot see the exit, but can still take it in fifth.

4.   Turn Four
Another long right hander entered in third, accelerated through fourth and exited in fifth.

5.   Turn Five
A right-left chicane that is entered in second gear, exited in third.

6.   Turn Six
A left hander where the approach is extremely bumpy.

7.   Turn Seven
This right hander is exited in fifth with the gentle left hander towards Eight taken flat out.

8.   Turn Eight
Not as fast as it looks as the corner suddenly tightens, with everybody using the exit kerb.

9.   Turn Nine
An off camber and downhill right-left chicane which always seems to gather particles of grit, whilst a high kerb awaits the unsuspecting at the second apex.

10.   Turn Ten
Hairpin like corner directly behind the pits and taken in second.

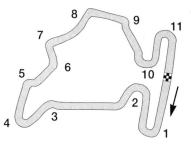

11. Turn Eleven

A long right hander that guards the pit straight. Plenty of action here as the cars first oversteer, turning to understeer by the time they exit on to the straight via the kerb.

Hungary – 10 Year Record

Year	1st	2nd	3rd	4th	5th	6th
1985	–	–	–	–	–	–
1986	Piquet (Williams)	Senna (Lotus)	Mansell (Williams)	Johansson (Ferrari)	Dumfries (Lotus)	Brundle (Tyrrell)
1987	Piquet (Williams)	Senna (Lotus)	Prost (McLaren)	Boutsen (Benetton)	Patrese (Brabham)	Warwick (Arrows)
1988	Senna (McLaren)	Prost (McLaren)	Boutsen (Benetton)	Berger (Ferrari)	Gugelmin (March)	Patrese (Williams)
1989	Mansell (Ferrari)	Senna (McLaren)	Boutsen (Williams)	Prost (McLaren)	Cheever (Arrows)	Piquet (Lotus)
1990	Boutsen (Williams)	Senna (McLaren)	Piquet (Benetton)	Patrese (Williams)	Warwick (Lotus)	Bernard (Lola)
1991	Senna (McLaren)	Mansell (Williams)	Patrese (Williams)	Berger (McLaren)	Alesi (Ferrari)	Capelli (Leyton House)
1992	Senna (McLaren)	Mansell (Williams)	Berger (McLaren)	Hakkinen (Lotus)	Brundle (Benetton)	Capelli (Ferrari)
1993	Hill (Williams)	Patrese (Benetton)	Berger (Ferrari)	Warwick (Footwork)	Brundle (Ligier)	Wendlinger (Sauber)
1994	Schumacher (Benetton)	Hill (Williams)	Verstappen (Benetton)	Brundle (McLaren)	Blundell (Tyrrell)	Panis (Ligier)

Imola

Lap Distance 3.132 miles/5.026 km
Race Distance 191.034 miles/307.439 km – 61 laps

1. Tamburello
First corner from the start. A left hander taken at speed, often still in sixth gear. Gained notoriety with the death of Ayrton Senna.

2. Villeneuve
No slower than Tamburello except that on exiting the car needs to be on the other side of the track with the driver beginning to get down through the gears to second ready for a sharp left hander. The combined change of speed and direction often finds drivers heading for the gravel trap at the left hander following Villeneuve.

3. Piratella
A somewhat blind left hander that is taken in fourth before changing quickly up to fifth to approach the bumpy left hander, downhill to Acque Minerale.

4. Acque Minerale
A very bumpy and uncomfortable chicane negotiated in second.

5. Variante Alfa
Fast chicane that can be tackled in third and certainly requires a third gear exit. Drivers tend to take more chance at this chicane because it does have a safe run-off area.

6. Rivazza
Requires hard braking down from sixth to second in order to tackle this right hander which is downhill and is taken in second. It opens out straight into a sharp left hander.

7. Variante Bassa
A very tricky right-left switchback which leads into Traguardo.

8. Traguardo
Almost as soon as the previous right-left flick is accomplished, Traguardo looms up as a left-right chicane that feeds the pits straight.

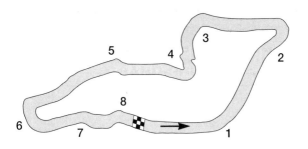

San Marino – 10 Year Record

Year	1st	2nd	3rd	4th	5th	6th
1985	de Angelis (Lotus)	Boutsen (Arrows)	Tambay (Renault)	Lauda (McLaren)	Mansell (Williams)	Johansson (Ferrari)
1986	Prost (McLaren)	Piquet (Williams)	Berger (Benetton)	Johansson (Ferrari)	Rosberg (McLaren)	Patrese (Benetton)
1987	Mansell (Williams)	Senna (Lotus)	Alboreto (Ferrari)	Johansson (McLaren)	Brundle (Zakspeed)	Nakajima (Lotus)
1988	Senna (McLaren)	Prost (McLaren)	Piquet (Lotus)	Boutsen (Benetton)	Berger (Ferrari)	Nannini (Benetton)
1989	Senna (McLaren)	Prost (McLaren)	Nannini (Benetton)	Boutsen (Williams)	Warwick (Arrows)	Palmer (Tyrrell)
1990	Patrese (Williams)	Berger (McLaren)	Nannini (Benetton)	Prost (Ferrari)	Piquet (Benetton)	Alesi (Tyrrell)
1991	Senna (McLaren)	Berger (McLaren)	Lehto (Dallara)	Martini (Minardi)	Hakkinen (Lotus)	Bsailey (Lotus)
1992	Mansell (Williams)	Patrese (Williams)	Senna (McLaren)	Brundle (Benetton)	Alboreto (Footwork)	Martini (Dallara)
1993	Prost (Williams)	Schumacher (Benetton)	Brundle (Ligier)	Lehto (Sauber)	Alliot (Larrousse)	Barbazza (Minardi)
1994	Schumacher (Benetton)	Nannini (Ferrari)	Hakkinen (McLaren)	Wendlinger (Sauber)	Katayama (Tyrrell)	Hill (Williams)

Interlagos

Lap Distance: 2.687 miles/4.323 km
Race Distance: 190.777 miles/306.933 km – 71 laps

---

1.   Senna's
Second gear entry, third gear exit

2.   Curva Do Sol
Flat out

3.   Subida Do Lago
There is a bumpy entrance to this tight left hander and a lot of cars manage to spin here.

4.   Curva do Laranja
Double apex right hander with an extremely bumpy entrance. Probably the most difficult corner on the circuit as it is downhill at speed. After going through the first apex in fourth, the car drifts out for the second apex and, on exiting at the top in third, another right hander is on top of you almost immediately as Pinheirinho approaches.

5.   Pinheirinho
Very tight left hander that should only be taken in second, exited in third and then up to fourth.

6.   Cotovello
No time to get into fifth as the car approaches Cotovello, a tight right hander that is taken in second, exited in third, climbing to fifth as the car makes for a left hander prior to turning for Mergulho.

7.   Mergulho
Taken in fourth before accelerating up to Subida (8) and Arquebancada (9) corners. These are both left handed, banked, and uphill before emerging on to the finishing straight.

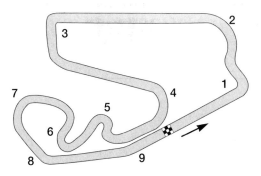

Brazil – 10 Year Record

Year	1st	2nd	3rd	4th	5th	6th
Jacarepagna						
1985	Prost (McLaren)	Alboreto (Ferrari)	de Angelis (Lotus)	Arnoux (Ferrari)	Tambay (Renault)	Laffite (Ligier)
1986	Piquet (Williams)	Senna (Lotus)	Laffite (Ligier)	Arnoux (Ligier)	Brundle Tyrrell	Berger Benetton
1987	Prost (McLaren)	Piquet (Williams)	Johnsson (McLaren)	Berger (Ferrari)	Boutsen (Benetton)	Mansell (Williams)
1988	Prost (McLaren)	Berger (Ferrari)	Piquet (Lotus)	Warwick (Arrows)	Alboreto (Ferrari)	Nsksjims (Lotus)
1989	Mansell (Ferrari)	Prost (McLaren)	Engelmin (March)	Herbert (Benetton)	Warwick (Arrows)	Nannini (Benetton)
Interlagos						
1990	Prost (Ferrari)	Berger (McLaren)	Senna (McLaren)	Mansell (Ferrari)	Boutsen (Williams)	Piquet (Benetton)
1991	Senna (McLaren)	Patrese (Williams)	Berger (McLaren)	Prost (Ferrari)	Piquet (Benetton)	Alesi (Ferrari)
1992	Mansell (Wiliams)	Patrese (Williams)	Schumacher (Benetton)	Alesi (Ferrari)	Capelli (Ferrari)	Alboreto (Footwork)
1993	Senna (McLaren)	Hill (Williams)	Schumacher (Benetton)	Herbert (Lotus)	Blundell (Ligier)	Zanardi (Lotus)
1994	Schumacher (Benetton)	Hill (Williams)	Alesi (Ferrari)	Barrichello (Jordan)	Katayama (Tyrrell)	Wendlinger (Sauber)

Magny-Cours

Lap Distance   2.640 miles/4.289 km
Race Distance   190.139 miles/305.998 km – 72 laps

1. **Grande Courbe**
    Because the bend leading to this long right hander is a left hander taken in sixth, it is difficult to get the car on the right line entering the bend, itself negotiated in fourth, before exiting to...

2. **Estoril**
    The long back straight, usually taken flat out.

3. **Adelaide**
    The straight finishes abruptly at Adelaide which is a 180 degree, second gear hairpin taking the vehicle back in the direction from which it has just come, towards...

4. **Nurburgring**
    A fast right-left that is cleared in fourth leads to Nurburgring which itself is not as tight as Adelaide but, nevertheless, is taken in second gear despite it being long and wide.

5. **Imola**
    From Nurburgring it's up quickly through the gears to fifth before changing down to meet the challenge of Imola, a right-left that protects...

6. **Chateaux d'Eau**
    A virtual 90 degree turn entered in second and exited in third on to a straight that allows the car to accelerate towards a second gear chicane.

7. **Lycee**
    Immediately following the chicane is the sharp Lycee right hander taken in third that opens into the pits straight.

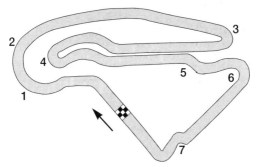

France – 10 Year Record

Year	1st	2nd	3rd	4th	5th	6th
La Castellet						
1985	Piquet (Brabham)	Rosberg (Williams)	Prost (McLaren)	Johansson (Ferrari)	de Angelis (Lotus)	Tambay (Renault)
1986	Mansell (Williams)	Prost (McLaren)	Piquet (Williams)	Rosberg (McLaren)	Arnoux (Tyrrell)	Laffite (Tyrrell)
1987	Mansell (Williams)	Piquet (Williams)	Prost (McLaren)	Senna (Lotus)	Fabi (Benetton)	Streiff (Tyrrell)
1988	Prost (McLaren)	Senna (McLaren)	Alboreto (Ferrari)	Berger (Ferrari)	Piquet (Lotus)	Nannini (Benetton)
1989	Prost (McLaren)	Mansell (Ferrari)	Patrese (Williams)	Alesi (Tyrrell)	Johansson (Onyx)	Grouillard (Ligier)
1990	Prost (Ferrari)	Capelli (March)	Senna (McLaren)	Piquet (Benetton)	Berger (McLaren)	Patrese (Williams)
Magny-Cours						
1991	Mansell (Williams)	Prost (Ferrari)	Senna (McLaren)	Alesi (Ferrari)	Patrese (Williams)	de Cesaris (Jordan)
1992	Mansell (Williams)	Patrese (Williams)	Brundle (Benetton)	Hakkinen (Lotus)	Comas (Ligier)	Herbert (Lotus)
1993	Prost (Williams)	Hill (Williams)	Schumacher (Benetton)	Senna (McLaren)	Brundle (Ligier)	Andretti (McLaren)
1994	Schumacher (Benetton)	Hill (Williams)	Berger (Ferrari)	Frentzen (Sauber)	Martini (Minardi)	de Cesaris (Sauber)

Monaco

Lap Distance   2.068 miles/3.328 km
Race Distance 161.298 miles/259.583 km – 78 laps

1. Virage de Sainte Devote
Approached from the pits in sixth but then it's down into third or fourth into this right hander.

2. Montee du Beau Rivage
Past Rosie's Bar in sixth and then it's over the crest of the hill and down to fourth as Virage Massenet beckons.

3. Virage Massenet
A long left hander, the car must be kept close to the inside kerbs.

4. Casino Square
A quick right hander that is taken in third before the downhill exit.

5. Virage Mirabeau
Approached downhill in fifth, the gear changes have to be fast to get into second for this bumpy right hander before exiting in third.

6. Virage Ancienne Gare
A left hand hairpin negotiated in second, the steering turned full lock, then right.

7. Virage du Portier
Another sharp right hander cleared in second.

8. Lowens Tunnel
With frightening noise and sparks, the cars change up to sixth.

9. Nouvelle Chicane
Left-right chicane taken in second.

10. Tabac
The most spectacular and glamourous part of the course alongside the harbour.

11. Swimming Pool
Lots of gear changes slow the cars.

12. Virage de la Rascasse
The slowest corner on the circuit which is taken in second, and then uphill to Virage Antony Noghes.

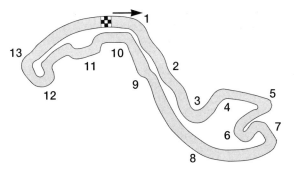

13. Virage Antony Noghes
Quickly up into third gear and back on to the pit straight.

Monaco – 10 Year Record

Year	1st	2nd	3rd	4th	5th	6th
1985	Prost (McLaren)	Alboreto (Ferrari)	de Angelis (Lotus)	de Cesaris (Ligier)	Warwick (Renault)	Laffite (Ligier)
1986	Prost (McLaren)	Rosberg (McLaren)	Senna (Lotus)	Mansell (Williams)	Arnoux (Ligier)	Laffite (Ligier)
1987	Senna (Lotus)	Piquet (Williams)	Alboreto (Ferrari)	Berger (Ferrari)	Palmer (Tyrrell)	Capelli (March)
1988	Prost (McLaren)	Berger (Ferrari)	Alboreto (Ferrari)	Warwick (Arrows)	Palmer (Tyrrell)	Patrese (Williams)
1989	Senna (McLaren)	Prost (McLaren)	Modena (Brabham)	Caffi (Dallara)	Alboreto (Tyrrell)	Brundle (Brabham)
1990	Senna (McLaren)	Alesi (Tyrrell)	Berger (McLaren)	Boutsen (Williams)	Caffi (Arrows)	Bernard (Lola)
1991	Senna (McLaren)	Mansell (Williams)	Alesi (Ferrari)	Moreno (Benetton)	Prost (Ferrari)	Pirro (Dallara)
1992	Senna (McLaren)	Mansell (Williams)	Patrese (Williams)	Schumacher (Benetton)	Brundle (Benetton)	Gachot (Larrousse)
1993	Senna (McLaren)	Hill (Williams)	Alesi (Ferrari)	Prost (Williams)	Fittipaldi (Minardi)	Brundle (Ligier)
1994	Schumacher (Benetton)	Brundle (McLaren)	Berger (Ferrari)	de Cesaris (Jordan)	Alesi (Ferrari)	Alboreto (Minardi)

Montreal

Lap Distance   2.753 miles/4.430 km
Race Distance   189.934 miles/305.668 km – 69 laps

1.   Island Hairpin

The track on Notre Dame Island can be quite windy. The circuit follows roads around the site of the World Fair which contains a number of manhole covers and is quite bumpy. The Grand Prix is the only race to take place on the course each year so the roads collect a great amount of grit which the wind shifts about causing severe grip problems that are constantly changing from place to place during the race.

2.   St. Lawrence River Straight

The start/finish straight runs alongside the Olympic Rowing Basin towards Island Hairpin which is taken in second and sometimes even first gear. Out of Island Hairpin there is just time to get up to fifth before a right-left chicane is taken in third. There is then a big right-hander to be taken in fifth. Almost immediately the cars are dropped into second for the next chicane, a left-right combination before the long back straight which runs adjacent to the St Lawrence River. Then a right-left chicane, which can be taken in third, beckons and then its flat out towards the second hairpin.

3.   Pits Hairpin

Pits Hairpin is a long loop which often sees a lot of overtaking action as it is quite wide. Out of Pits Hairpin the cars have yet another chicane to negotiate before they can approach the home straight which is guarded by one final chicane.

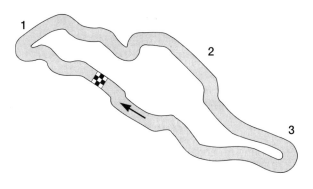

Canada – 10 Year Record

Year	1st	2nd	3rd	4th	5th	6th
Montreal						
1985	Alboreto (Ferrari)	Johnsson (Ferrari)	Prost (McLaren)	Rosberg (Williams)	de Angelis (Lotus)	Mansell (Williams)
1986	Mansell (Williams)	Prost (McLaren)	Piquet (Williams)	Rosberg (McLaren)	Senna (Lotus)	Arnoux (Ligier)
1987	–	–	–	–	–	–
1988	Senna (McLaren)	Prost (McLaren)	Boutsen (Benetton)	Piquet (Lotus)	Capelli (March)	Palmer (Tyrrell)
1989	Boutsen (Williams)	Patrese (Williams)	de Cesaris (Dallara)	Piquet (Lotus)	Arnoux (Ligier)	Caffi (Dallara)
1990	Senna (McLaren)	Piquet (Benetton)	Mansell (Ferrari)	Berger (McLaren)	Prost (Ferrari)	Warwick (Lotus)
1991	Piquet (Benetton)	Modena (Tyrrell)	Patrese (Williams)	de Cesaris (Jordan)	Gachot (Jordan)	Mansell (Williams)
1992	Berger (Ferrari)	Schumacher (Benetton)	Alesi (Ferrari)	Wendlinger (March)	de Cesaris (Tyrrell)	Comas (Ligier)
1993	Prost (Williams)	Schumacher (Benetton)	Hill (Williams)	Berger (Ferrari)	Brundle (Ligier	Wendlinger (Sauber)
1994	Schumacher (Benetton)	Hill (Williams)	Alesi (Ferrari)	Berger (Ferrari)	Coulthard (Williams)	Lehto (Benetton)

Monza

Lap Distance 3.602 miles/5.794 km
Race Distance 191.009 miles/307.398 km – 53 laps

1. Variante Goodyear

This is approached at some 190mph due to the long, wide pit straight that precedes it. It is a very fast but bumpy left-right-left-right second gear chicane.

2. Curva Grande

A very bumpy longish right hander that is hard work on the steering. Drivers invariably use the kerb at its exit.

3. Variante della Roggia

The breaking area prior to entering this left-right chicane is both bumpy and slippy.

4. Curvo di Lesmos

Contentious sharp right handers that Damon Hill criticised as "Too dangerous even for a F3000 car because there is not a sufficient run off area due to it being a part of the Royal Park". Invariably taken at speed in fifth and exited in sixth gear.

5. Curva del Serraglio

A long straight that means the driver approaches the next chicane at speeds approaching 200mph.

6. Curva del Vialone

Drivers hope their brakes are in good order as they approach this left hander braking from 200 mph in sixth gear to fourth gear at the 100 metre board. Then onto...

6. Variante Ascari

The second part of the chicane quickly flicking right, then left. Exited in fifth on to the Rettifilio Centro straight.

7. Curvo Parabolica

A long, looping right hander that is entered from the Rettifilio straight in fourth before moving in to fifth gear as the bend begins to open up and exited in sixth. Known for generating a great deal of understeer.

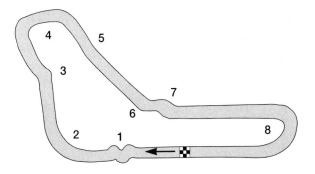

Italy – 10 Year Record

Year	1st	2nd	3rd	4th	5th	6th
1985	Prost (McLaren)	Piquet (Brabham)	Senna (Lotus)	Surer (Brabham)	Johansson (Ferrari)	de Angelis (Lotus)
1986	Piquet (Williams)	Mansell (Williams)	Johansson (Ferrari)	Rosberg (McLaren)	Berger (Benetton)	Jones (Lola)
1987	Piquet (Williams)	Senna (Lotus)	Mansell (Williams)	Berger (Ferrari)	Boutsen (Benetton)	Johansson (McLaren)
1988	Berger (Ferrari)	Alboreto (Ferrari)	Cheever (Arrows)	Warwick (Arrows)	Capelli (March)	Boutsen (Benetton)
1989	Prost (McLaren)	Berger (Ferrari)	Boutsen (Williams)	Patrese (Williams)	Alesi (Tyrell)	Brundle (Brabham)
1990	Senna (McLaren)	Prost (Ferrari)	Berger (McLaren)	Mansell (Ferrari)	Patrese (Williams)	Nakajima (Tyrrell)
1991	Mansell (Williams)	Senna (McLaren)	Prost (Ferrari)	Berger (McLaren)	Schumacher (Benetton)	Piquet (Benetton)
1992	Senna (McLaren)	Brundle (Benetton)	Schumacher (Benetton)	Berger (McLaren)	Patrese (Williams)	de Cesaris (Tyrell)
1993	Hill (Williams)	Alesi (Ferrari)	Andretti (McLaren)	Wendlinger (Sauber)	Patrese (Benetton)	Comas (Larrousse)
1994	Hill (Williams)	Berger (Ferrari)	Verstappen (Benetton)	Barrichello (Jordan)	Brundle (McLaren)	Coulthard (Williams)

Nurburgring

Lap Distance   2.822 miles/5.794 kms

The Grand Prix circuit will play home to its first Formula One race since 1985 when the F1 circuit lap record was set by Niki Lauda in a McLaren at 1m 22.81s. The circuit has been revised since then and a lap record of 1m 21.553s was set by Fabi in a Jaguar in 1991.

The original circuit played host to 23 German Grand Prix plus one European Grand Prix in 1984.

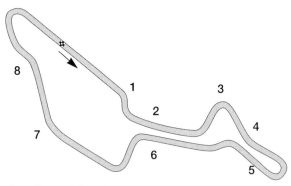

1. **Castrol Bend**
2. **Sachs Passage**
3. **Vavoline Curve**
4. **Foro Curve**
5. **Dunlope Corner**
6. **Yokohama Curve**
7. **Bit Curve**
8. **Veedol Curve**

European – 10 Year Record

Year	1st	2nd	3rd	4th	5th	6th
Brands Hatch						
1985	Mansell (Williams)	Senna (Lotus)	Rosberg (Williams)	Prost (McLaren)	de Angelis (Lotus)	Boutsen (Arrows)

1986-1992 No European Grand Prix held.

Year	1st	2nd	3rd	4th	5th	6th
Donington						
1993	Senna (McLaren)	Hill (Williams)	Prost (Williams)	Herbert (Lotus)	Patrese (Benetton)	Barbazza (Minardi)
Jerez						
1994	Schumacher (Benetton)	Hill (Williams)	Hakkinen (McLaren)	Irvine (Jordan)	Berger (Ferrari)	Frentsen (Sauber)

Silverstone

Lap Distance   3.142 miles/5.23 km
Race Distance   188.52 miles/313.80 km – 59 laps

1.   Copse
Previously negotiated in fifth at 250kph, it is now taken in third at approximately 150kph after safety alterations, with quick changes back to sixth before...

2.   Maggotts
Dropping down to fifth for Maggotts which guards the entrance to...

3.   Becketts
A left hander entered in fourth at 280 kph dropping to about 175kph for the exit to...

4.   Chapel
The last of the series of left-right-left-right-left bends leading to...

5.   Hangar Straight
The fastest part of the circuit at 300kph.

6.   Stowe
Previously taken at about 175kph it has been slowed to about 120kph as a result of being made much tighter.

7.   Vale
The cars go through at something like 260kph with good overtaking opportunities and a second gear, sharp left into...

8.   Club
A right hand corner with very good overtaking opportunities.

9.   Abbey
Previously taken flat out, alterations make this a third gear left-right bend.

10.   Bridge Corner
Now taken in fifth and about 250kph, 50kph slower than previously.

11-13. Priory/Brooklands/Luffield
A series of flicks coming so close on one another that ensures it is the slowest part of the circuit before the cars emerge into...

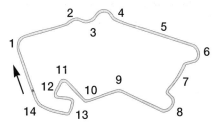

14. Woodcote

A quick dash to the finishing straight.

Gt Britain – 10 Year Record

Year	1st	2nd	3rd	4th	5th	6th
Silverstone						
1985	Prost (McLaren)	Alboreto (Ferrari)	Laffite (Ligier)	Piquet (Brabham)	Warwick (Renault)	Surer (Brabham)
Brands Hatch						
1986	Mansell (Williams)	Piquet (Williams)	Prost (McLaren)	Arnoux (Ligier)	Brundle (Tyrrell)	Streiff (Tyrrell)
Silverstone						
1987	Mansell (Williams)	Piquet (Williams)	Senna (Lotus)	Nakajima (Lotus)	Warwick (Arrows)	Fabi (Benetton)
1988	Senna (McLaren)	Mansell (Williams)	Nannini (Benetton)	Gugelmin (March)	Piquet (Lotus)	Warwick (Arrows)
1989	Prost (McLaren)	Mansell (Ferrari)	Nannini (Benetton)	Piquet (Lotus)	Martini (Minardi)	Perez-Sala (Minardi)
1990	Prost (Ferrari)	Boutsen (Williams)	Senna (McLaren)	Bernard (Lola)	Piquet (Benetton)	Suzuki (Lola)
1991	Mansell (Williams)	Berger (McLaren)	Prost (Ferrari)	Senna (McLaren)	Piquet (Benetton)	Gachot (Jordan)
1992	Mansell (Williams)	Patrese (Williams)	Brundle (Benetton)	Schumacher (Benetton)	Berger (McLaren)	Hakkinen (Lotus)
1993	Prost (Williams)	Schumacher (Benetton)	Patrese (Benetton)	Herbert (Lotus)	Senna (McLaren)	Warwick (Footwork)
1994	Hill (Williams)	Alesi (Ferrari)	Hakkinen (McLaren)	Barrichello (Jordan)	Coulthard (Williams)	Katayama (Tyrrell)

Spa

Lap Distance   4.33 miles/6.968 km
Race Distance   190.671 miles/306.854 km – 44 laps

1.   La Source
The corner comes very quickly after the start of the race and is a sharp right hander taken in second.

2.   Eau Rouge
Entered in sixth gear, it went sharply downhill and then uphill left, right, and left. In its modified form it cuts sharp left at the bottom of the hill, curving back on a right hander for the long Kemmel straight.

3.   Les Combes
Good overtaking possibilities exist at this right-left chicane due to the good run-off areas. The right-left combination is taken in third and exited in fourth.

4.   Malmedy
A virtual hairpin which, due to being off camber, causes cars all sorts of steering problems. Taken in second, exited in third.

5.   Le Pouhon
Also off camber, this double left hander is entered in fifth and exited in sixth.

6.   Les Fanges
A right left chicane where the entry is made in third, up to fourth in the middle section and exited via the use of the kerb.

7.   Stavelot
A double right hander that is fast as it is downhill. Entered in third with fourth being engaged in the middle but it is bumpy and cars tend to skip about a bit.

8.   Blanchimont
A long sweeping lefthander leading to...

9.   Bus Stop
A sharp right-left-right that slows the cars right down before emerging on to the pit straight.

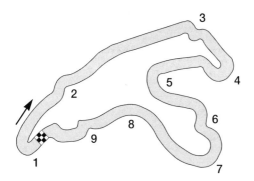

Belgium – 10 Year Record

Year	1st	2nd	3rd	4th	5th	6th
1985	Senna (Lotus)	Mansell (Williams)	Prost (McLaren)	Rosberg (Williams)	Piquet (Brabham)	Warwick (Renault)
1986	Mansell (Williams)	Senna (Lotus)	Johansson (Ferrari)	Alboreto (Ferrari)	Laffite (Ligier)	Prost (McLaren)
1987	Prost (McLaren)	Johansson (McLaren)	de Cesaris (Brabham)	Cheever (Arrows)	Nakajima (Lotus)	Arnoux (Ligier)
1988	Senna (McLaren)	Prost (McLaren)	Capelli (March)	Piquet (Lotus)	Warwick (Arrows)	Cheever (Arrows)
1989	Senna (McLaren)	Prost (McLaren)	Mansell (Ferrari)	Boutsen (Williams)	Nannini (Benetton)	Warwick (Arrows)
1990	Senna (McLaren)	Prost (Ferrari)	Berger (McLaren)	Nannini (Benetton)	Piquet (Benneton)	Gugelmin (March)
1991	Senna (McLaren)	Berger (McLaren)	Piquet (Benetton)	Moreno (Benetton)	Patrese (Williams)	Blundell (Brabham)
1992	Schumacher (Benetton)	Mansell (Williams)	Patrese (Williams)	Brundle (Benetton)	Senna (McLaren)	Hakkinen (Lotus)
1993	Hill (Williams)	Schumacher (Benetton)	Prost (Williams)	Senna (McLaren)	Herbert (Lotus)	Patrese (Benetton)
1994	Hill (Williams)	Hakkinen (McLaren)	Verstappen (Benetton)	Coulthard (Williams)	Blundell (Tyrrell)	Morbidelli (Arrows)

Suzuka

Lap Distance   3.64 miles/5.858km
Race Distance   193.117 miles/310.791km – 53 laps

1.   Turn One
Approached from the short start/finish straight flat out in sixth with a change down to fifth.

2.   Turn Two
Much tighter than the first corner and can only be negotiated in fourth.

3.   The S Curves
Left-right-left-right combination that severely taxes any car that is not well balanced. Can usually be taken in fourth.

4.   Dunlop Curve
On exiting the S Curves it is immediately up to fifth for a long left hander. Extremely bumpy with plenty of understeer.

5.   Degner Curve
A very tight right hander that is entered in fourth, down to third as the second part of the corner becomes tighter still and then generally exited with the use of the kerb. Then it is up to fourth and fifth to go under the bridge where the course crosses itself.

6.   Hairpin
Is guarded by a short right hander which somewhat slows the cars but then they have to get down very quickly to second gear for the hairpin.

7.   Spoon Curve
Approached via a long looping right hander in sixth gear before entering the actual left hander in fourth. It tightens up forcing the cars to take third gear as they drift to the outside. The cars tend to understeer but it is important to get the exit right as it leads on to the fastest part of the track over the bridge.

8.   "130 R"
A very fast left hander which only slows the cars down to fifth gear.

9.   Chicane
The Chicane guards the entrance to the finishing straight. The right-left combination is taken in second before third gear is snatched for the final right hander.

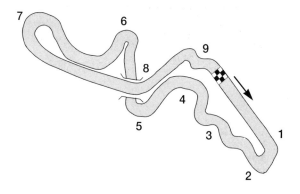

Japan – 10 Year Record

Year	1st	2nd	3rd	4th	5th	6th
1985	–	–	–	–	–	–
1986	–	–	–	–	–	–
1987	Berger (Ferrari)	Senna (Lotus)	Johansson (McLaren)	Alboreto (Ferrari)	Boutsen (Benetton)	Nakajima (Lotus)
1988	Senna (McLaren)	Prost (McLaren)	Boutsen (Benetton)	Berger (Ferrari)	Nannini (Benetton)	Patrese (Williams)
1989	Nannini (Benetton)	Patrese (Williams)	Boutsen (Williams)	Piquet (Lotus)	Brundle (Brabham)	Warwick (Arrows)
1990	Piquet (Benetton)	Moreno (Benetton)	Suzuki (Lola)	Patrese (Williams)	Boutsen (Williams)	Nakajima (Tyrell)
1991	Berger (McLaren)	Senna (McLaren)	Patrese (Williams)	Prost (Ferrari)	Blundell (Brabham)	Modena (Tyrrell)
1992	Patrese (Williams)	Berger (McLaren)	Brundle (Benetton)	de Cesaris (Tyrrell)	Alesi (Ferrari)	Fittipaldi (Minardi)
1993	Senna (McLaren)	Prost (Williams)	Hakkinen (McLaren)	Hill (Williams)	Barrichello (Jordan)	Irvine (Jordan)
1994	Hill (Williams)	Schumacher (Benetton)	Alesi (Ferrari)	Mansell (Williams)	Irvine (Jordan)	Frentzen (Sauber)

Track Records

The lap records for each of the circuits nominated for the 1995 season are
listed below. In several cases the times given are for circuits where the track
has been revised, which makes direct comparisions a little pointless.

Adelaide (Australia)	Damon Hill Williams	GB	1m 15.381s 112.172mph/180.523kph	1993
Aida (Pacific)	Michael Scumacher Benetton	Ger	1m 14.023s 111.872mph/180.041kph	1994
Buenos Aires (Arg)†	Nelon Piquet Brabham	Brz	1m 45.287s 124.728mph/204.059kph	1981
Catalunya (Spain)	Michael Scumacher Benetton	Ger	1m 20.989s 131.113mph/211.006kph	1993
Estoril (Portugal)*	David Coulthard Williams	GB	1m 22.446s 118.296mph/190.379kph	1994
Hockenheim (Germany)	Michael Scumacher Benetton	Ger	1m 41.859 143.700mph/241.498kph	1993
Hungaroring (Hungary)	Nigel Mansell Williams	GB	1m 18.308s 113.349mph/182.418kph	1992
Imola (San Marino)	Damon Hill Williams	GB	1m 24.335s 133.682mph/215.141kph	1994
Interlagos (Brazil)	Nigel Mansell Williams	GB	1m 17.578s 122.865mph/197.731kph	1992
Magny-Cours (France)	Nigel Mansell Williams	GB	1m 17.070s 123.355mph/198.521kph	1992
Monaco	Michael Scumacher Benetton	Ger	1m 21.076s 91.821mph/147.772kph	
Montreal (Can)	Michael Scumacher Benetton	Ger	1m 21.500s 121.591mph/195.681kph	1993
Monza (Italy)	Damon Hill Williams	GB	1m 25.985s 150.985mph/242.968kph	1993
Nurburgring (Eur)†	Niki Lauda McLaren	Aut	1m 22.81s 123.415mph/197kph	1985
Silverstone (GB)*	Damon Hill Williams	GB	1m 27.100s 129.875mph/209.014kph	1994

Spa (Bel)*	Damon Hill Williams	GB	1m 57.117s 134.500mph/215.200kph	1994
Suzuka (Japan)	Nigel Mansell Williams	GB	1m 40.646s 130.332mph/209.749kph	1992

* Record for revised circuit. † Record for unrevised (pre-1995) circuit

Race Diary '95

Listed below are dates and venues for the 1995 Formula One season which consists of 16 races. Although the dates and venues of these races were correct at the time of writing they are subject to change and alteration. The Circuit Directory details one extra track – this is the Hungarian circuit at Hungaroring which is the reserve track for the season and will be used should it prove impossible to stage a Grand Prix at one of the designated circuits.

Date	Grand Prix	Country	Circuit
March 26	Brazilian	Brazil	Interlagos
April 9	Argentinian	Argentina	Buenos Aires
April 30	San Marino	San Marino	Imola
May 14	Spanish	Spain	Catalunya
May 28	Monaco	Monaco	Monaco
June 11	Canadian	Canada	Montreal
July 2	French	France	Magny-Cours
July 16	British	England	Silverstone
July 30	German	Germany	Hockenheim
August 13	*Hungarian*	*Hungary*	*Hungaroring**
August 27	Belgian	Belgium	Spa
September 10	Italian	Italy	Monza
September 24	Portuguese	Portugal	Estoril
October 1	European	Germany	Nurburgring
October 22	Pacific	Japan	Aida
October 29	Japanese	Japan	Suzuka
November 12	Australian	Australia	Adelaide

* Reserve Grand Prix

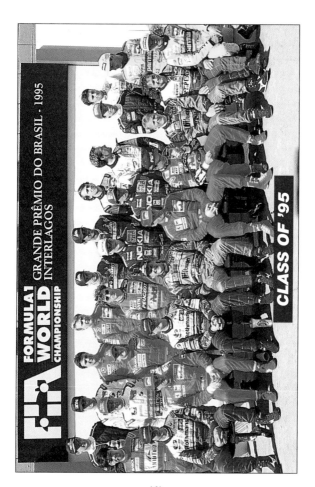

MILD SEVEN BENETTON RENAULT

1 – Michael Schumacher (Germany)

2 – Johnny Herbert (GB)

ROTHMANS WILLIAMS RENAULT

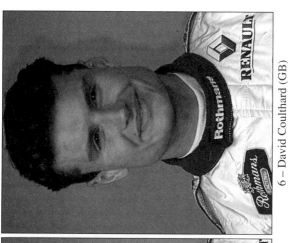

6 – David Coulthard (GB)

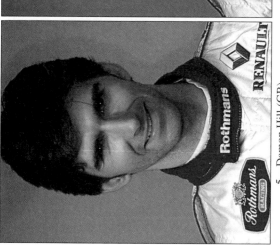

5 – Damon Hill (GB)

MARLBORO McLAREN MERCEDES

8 – Mika Hakkinen (Finland)

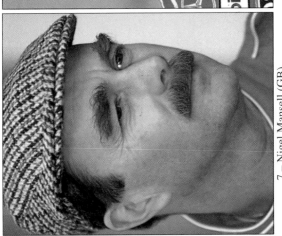

7 – Nigel Mansell (GB)

FERRARI

28 – Gerhard Berger (Austria)

27 – Jean Alesi (France)

NOKIA TYRRELL YAMAHA

4 – Mika Salo (Finland)

3 – Ukyo Katayama (Japan)

ARROWS HART

9 – Gianni Morbidelli (Italy)

10 – Takachiho Inoue (Japan)

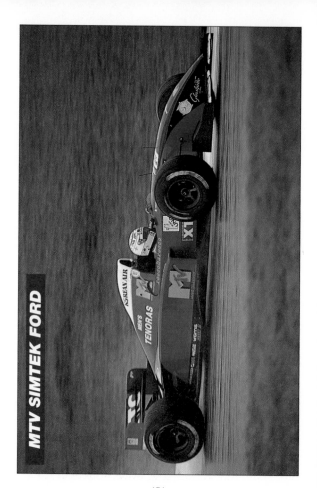

MTV SIMTEK FORD

12 – Jos Verstappen (Holland)

11 – Hideki Noda (Japan)

TOTAL JORDAN PEUGEOT

15 – Eddie Irvine (GB)

14 – Rubens Barrichello (Brazil)

PACIFIC TEAM LOTUS

17 – Andrea Montermini (Italy)

16 – Bertrand Gachot (Belgium)

LARROUSSE FORD

20 – Eric Bernard (France)

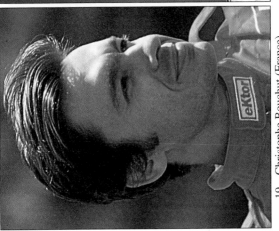

19 – Christophe Bouchut (France)

FORTI CORSE FORD

22 – Roberto Moreno (Brazil)

21 – Pedro Paulo Diniz (Brazil)

MINARDI FORD

24 – Luca Badoer (Italy)

23 – Pier-Luigi Martini (Italy)

26 – Olivier Panis (France)

25 – Aguri Suzuki (Japan)

RED BULL SAUBER FORD

30 – Heinz-Harald Frentzen (Germany)

29 – Karl Wendlinger (Austria)

11 – Mimmo Schiattarella (Italy) – Simtek

7 – Mark Blundell (GB) – McLaren

The Shape of things to come?

25 – Martin Brundle (GB) – Ligier

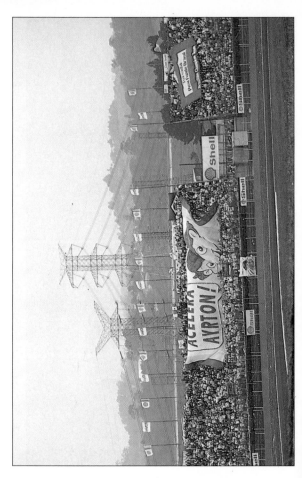